CAMRA'S BOOK OF

BEER
KNOWLEDGE

Published by the Campaign for Real Ale Ltd.
230 Hatfield Road
St Albans
Hertfordshire AL1 4LW

www.camra.org.uk/books

© Campaign for Real Ale 2011
Text © Jeff Evans
First published 2004
Reprinted with updates and amendments 2007
Second edition 2011

ISBN 978-1-85249-292-2

A CIP catalogue record for this book is available from the British Library.
Printed and bound in Slovenia by Latitude Press Ltd.

Head of Publishing: Simon Hall
Project Editor: Katie Hunt
Editorial Assistance: Emma Haines
Design/Typography: Linda Storey
Head of Marketing: Tony Jerome

CAMRA'S BOOK OF

Essential Wisdom
for the
Discerning Drinker

Jeff Evans

BOOKS

Opening Salvo

*'A man who doesn't care about the beer he drinks
may as well not care about the bread he eats'.*

The words with which Michael Jackson opened his magnum opus, *The World Guide to Beer*, in 1977, so embarking on a journey to raise the appreciation of beer to a whole new level. The book changed many lives.

Pubs Featuring in Every Edition of the *Good Beer Guide*

The *Good Beer Guide* is CAMRA's flagship publication. For nearly 40 years it has led British beer lovers to the pubs serving the best traditional ale, as well as providing valuable information about the country's breweries and the many beers they produce. Here is a list of ever-present pubs*:

Buckingham Arms, Westminster, London SW1
Fisherman's Tavern, Broughty Ferry, Tayside**
New Inn, Kilmington, Devon
Queen's Head, Newton, Cambridgeshire
Roscoe Head, Liverpool, Merseyside
Square & Compass, Worth Matravers, Dorset
Star, Netherton, Northumberland
Star Tavern, Belgravia, London SW1

*To 2012 edition. **Not in the first edition as no Scottish pubs were entered.

The Cycling Pioneer

Henry Wadworth, founder of Wadworth's brewery in Devizes, Wiltshire, claims to have been one of the first cyclists in Britain. In his memoirs, he recalls having a bicycle made in April 1869, shortly after the invention had been introduced to the UK. The primitive vehicle had 30-inch wheels and iron tyres. To put it to the test, Wadworth rode from Knightsbridge, London, all the way to Bath, a journey that took two and a half days. 'I was one of the first to ride a bicycle down the Bath road and I remember being pleased with the sensation I caused,' he wrote.

Barrels, Casks and Kegs

When your bartender says he's just off to 'change the barrel', it's extremely unlikely that he'll be doing exactly that. A barrel is actually an imperial measure of 36 gallons (approximately 164 litres) and, such is the demand for greater choice and faster turnover of beers, very few barrels are rolled out into the pub trade these days. The proper term for a real ale container is a cask (hence the term 'cask-conditioned ale'), and casks are now generally limited to 18-gallon (kilderkin) and 9-gallon (firkin) sizes (for a full list of cask sizes see page 23). A keg is a different kind of beer container, devised for holding and dispensing pressurized beer. A commonly used keg size is 11 gallons (approximately 50 litres).

Some Popular Beer Glass Shapes

Shaker
Used for ales, particularly in the USA. Originally devised as part of the kit for 'shaking' and serving cocktails.

Tulip
Used for ales, particularly in the UK. A shapely, more aesthetically pleasing version of the straight 'sleeve' pint glass.

Nonic
Used for ales, particularly in the UK. The bulge is intended to prevent the rims chipping in the glass washer (hence 'no nick').

Weissbier Glass
Used for German-style wheat beers. The extended height and tapering shape allow the thick foam to be captured at the top.

Chalice or Goblet
Used for strong ales, particularly in Belgium. The shape and name echo the religious origins of Trappist and Abbey beers.

Pilsner Glass
Used for true pilsner lagers, particularly in Germany. The tapered shape allows deep foam to collect at the top.

Stemmed Tulip
Used for strong ales, particularly in Belgium. The curved shape both retains foam and allows aromas to be accentuated.

Seidel
Used for helles and other lagers, particularly in Germany. The thick glass and handle help to keep the beer cold.

Five Facts About Barley

Barley has been cultivated by man for around 10,000 years and used to make beer for much of that time.

Barley for brewing grows in two varieties, two-row and six-row, based on the number of seeds on the stalk.

The long whiskers that surround the seeds are known as awns.

Barley is also differentiated by the time of the year in which it is sown – hence winter barleys (sown in the autumn and grown through winter to be harvested in summer) and spring barley (sown in the spring and harvested in late summer).

There are numerous strains of brewing barley, the best known British strains including Maris Otter, Optic, Fanfare, Halcyon, Pipkin, Alexis, Chariot and Pearl.

Editors of CAMRA's *Good Beer Guide*

1974	John Hanscomb	**1989–90**	Andrea Gillies
1975–7	Michael Hardman	**1991–8**	Jeff Evans
1978–83	Roger Protz	**1999**	Jonathan Preece
1984–8	Neil Hanson	**2000–**	Roger Protz

The Golden Triangle

The development of modern day lager beer can be traced back to three important brewing cities, and three innovative brewers who worked within them during the same era. These pioneers were Gabriel Sedlmayr of Spaten, in Munich, who, in the 1830s, collaborated with Anton Dreher of Vienna, to embrace emerging technology and better understand the science and practice of cold fermentation and lagering. The third brewer was Josef Groll, who, in 1842, developed the first blond lager in Pilsen, Czech Republic. The cities of Munich, Vienna and Pilsen therefore form what has become known to brewing historians as 'The Golden Triangle'.

Famous Beer Advertising Slogans

'After one you'll do anything well' .... Whitbread Tankard
'Australian for beer' .... Foster's
'Australians wouldn't give a XXXX for
   anything else' .... Castlemaine XXXX
'Bang on!' .... Wells Bombardier
'Bitte, ein Bit' .... Bitburger
'Follow the bear' .... Hofmeister
'Good for you' .... Guinness
'Good things come to those who wait' .... Guinness
'He who thinks Australian, drinks Australian' .... Foster's
'I bet he drinks ...' .... Carling Black Label
'I'm only here for the beer' .... Double Diamond
'It looks good, tastes good and
   by golly it does you good' .... Mackeson
'It's blended ... it's splendid' .... Pabst Blue Ribbon
'Lose the carbs, not the taste' .... Michelob Ultra
'No fokker comes close' .... Shepherd Neame Spitfire
'Probably the best lager in the world' .... Carlsberg
'Reassuringly expensive' .... Stella Artois
'Refreshes the parts other beers cannot reach' .... Heineken
'Sharp to the bottom of the glass' .... Harp
'Some things get better given longer' .... Greene King Abbot Ale
'The amber nectar' .... Foster's
'The beer that made Milwaukee famous' .... Schlitz
'The coldest tasting beer in the world' .... Coors Lite
'The Champagne of bottled beer' .... Miller High Life
'The cream of Manchester' .... Boddingtons
'The king of beers' .... Budweiser
'The not so traditional ale' .... Greene King Old Speckled Hen
'The one and only' .... Newcastle Brown Ale
'The pint that thinks it's a quart' .... Whitbread Trophy
'Wassup?' .... Budweiser
'We only let you drink it when it's ready' .... Grolsch
'What your right arm's for' .... Courage Tavern
'Whatever you do, take Pride' .... Fuller's London Pride
'Where there's life, there's Bud' .... Budweiser
'Works wonders' .... Double Diamond

Five Great Beer Bars in Brussels

Bier Circus, 57 Rue de l'Enseignement
Appealing corner café, with a reputation for beer and food pairing.

Delirium Café, 4a Impasse de la Fidelité
Often bustling cellar bar, with more than 2,000 bottled beers.

Moeder Lambic, 68 Rue de Savoie
Lambics and more, plus a choice of gourmet cheeses.

Mort Subite, 7 Rue Montagnes-aux-Herbes Potagères
Mirrored institution after which the Mort Subite beer range is named.

Poechenellekelder, 5 Rue du Chêne
Guardian of the Mannekin Pis, housing some of the little boy's clothes.

Gravity, Plato and Balling

Original gravity (OG), like its continental equivalents, degrees Plato and degrees Balling, provides a rough indicator of the strength of a beer. As a reading of the weight of the wort prior to fermentation against the weight of water, it indicates the amount of fermentable sugars in the brew before the yeast sets to work, and this can be used to calculate the approximate finishing strength. For instance, a beer with an OG of 1.040 (water has a gravity of 1.000), will probably turn out at around 4% ABV. However, by allowing the beer to ferment for longer or shorter periods, the brewer can make the beer a bit weaker or stronger than this.

Balling and Plato come up with the same indicators in a different way, by measuring the density, rather than the weight, of the wort. A beer with 10 degrees Balling or Plato contains 10 per cent solid materials (i.e. dissolved sugars). Balling is named in honour of Czech scientist Karl (or Carl) Balling, while Plato takes its name from Fritz Plato, a German who adapted Balling's work. The Balling and Plato scales are very close but are not exactly the same, because of a slight difference in the temperature at which each is calculated. To convert a degrees Plato or Balling figure to an approximate original gravity, multiply by four. Hence a 10 degree Balling/Plato beer would have an original gravity of 1.040.

Brewers of the Year

Since 1995, the All Party Parliamentary Beer Group has presented an award to its 'Brewer of the Year'. The recipients to date are as follows:

Year	Brewer	Brewery
1995	Tony Skipper	McMullen
1996	Paul Bayley	Marston's
1997	Paul Theakston	Black Sheep
1998	Alistair Heeley	Greene King
1999	Reg Drury	Fuller's
2000	Stuart Noble	Bass
2001	Miles Jenner	Harveys
2002	Ken Don	Young's
2003	Mike Powell-Evans	Adnams
2004	Giles Dennis	Lees
2005	Jeremy Moss	Wychwood
2006	Steve Fielding	Thwaites
2007	Steve Wellington	White Shield
2008	Ian Dixon	Shepherd Neame
2009	Roger Ryman	St Austell
2010	Stefano Cossi	Thornbridge
2011	Stuart Howe	Sharp's

Pink Boots, Barley's Angels and Project Venus

Created 'to inspire, encourage and empower women to advance their careers in the beer industry through networking and education', the Pink Boots Society is an association of female, mostly American brewers. Its members work for breweries, large and small, across the USA and also in other countries, including Canada, the UK and Australia. Its active consumer wing, deftly labelled Barley's Angels, is committed to educating and enthusing female beer drinkers – described as 'an often under-recognized demographic group' – around the world by staging a variety of tastings, talks and seminars. Inspired by the efforts of Pink Boots, a collection of female brewers in the UK and Ireland founded Project Venus in 2011, using collaborative brewing to raise the profile and highlight the skills of women working in beer.

A Chronology of Notable British Brewery Openings

1698	Shepherd Neame	1882	Brains
1777	Hall & Woodhouse	1890	Banks's*
1790	Harveys	1915	Holden's
1794	Palmers	1965	Traquair
1799	Greene King	1977	Blackawton
1807	Thwaites	1978	Butcombe
1827	McMullen		Ringwood*
	Theakston	1979	Broughton
1828	Jennings*		Cotleigh
	Lees	1980	Exmoor
1830	Felinfoel	1981	Crouch Vale
1834	Marston's		Woodforde's
1838	Robinson's	1982	Burton Bridge
1845	Fuller's		Mauldons
1847	John Smith's**		Pilgrim
1849	Everards	1983	Wychwood
	Holt's	1984	Cropton
	Hook Norton	1985	Harviestoun
1851	St Austell		Titanic
1858	Taylor	1987	Caledonian
1863	Arkell's		Hop Back
	Hydes	1988	Daleside
1865	Donnington	1990	Cains
	Moorhouse's		Kelham Island
1872	Adnams	1991	Hambleton
1874	Batemans	1992	Black Sheep
	Okells	1994	Sharp's****
1875	Wadworth	2000	Meantime
1876	Wells***	2003	Copper Dragon
1877	Batham	2005	Thornbridge
1878	Elgood's	2007	BrewDog

Dates are declared in different ways by breweries. Some refer to the year the business was established; others reflect the age of the brewery itself, which previously may have been run by other companies.

*Now part of Marston's (formerly Wolverhampton & Dudley).

**Now part of Heineken UK.

***Now operating as Wells & Young's.   ****Now part of Molson Coors

Gluten-free Beers

Recognizing that an increasing number of people suffer from coeliac's disease, triggered by the presence of gluten in their diet, a number of brewers now produce gluten-free beers. These often substitute malted barley with other cereals, including sorghum, maize and buckwheat. Here are some of the most prominent gluten-free beers in production.

Beer	Brewery	Country
Against the Grain	Wold Top	UK
Bard's	Bard's Tale	USA
Celia	Zatec	Czech Republic
Free Aglut	Heineken	Italy
GFA	Hambleton	UK
Daura	Estrella Damm	Spain
GFL	Hambleton	UK
G-Free	St Peter's	UK
Schnitzer Bräu	Schnitzer Bräu	Germany

There is also a range of gluten-free beers promoted under the Green's label and contract brewed for this Yorkshire-based company.

The Healing Power of Beer

When President Obama needed to make amends for a rash comment, he reached for a beer. In 2009, a white Massachusetts police sergeant, Joseph Crowley, had arrested a black Harvard University professor, Henry Louis Gates, for apparently breaking into a house. It turned out to be his home and Gates' treatment at the hands of the police drew questions of racism. The President – somewhat hastily, his detractors decided – criticized the police handling of the situation but then looked for a way to extricate himself from a difficult situation, hoping to reconcile the conflicting parties. His answer lay in a friendly, social drink. He invited the police officer and the lecturer to join him in a glass of beer at The White House – not a bottle of wine, a cup of tea or a mug of coffee: *a glass of beer*. In such circumstances, Obama realized only beer would do. Such is the healing power of our favourite drink. As for the beers consumed, Gates chose Samuel Adams Lite, Crowley opted for Blue Moon and Obama went for Bud Lite. Ah well, nobody's perfect.

Important Dates in Brewing History

c.4000 BC .... Beer is being produced in the Middle East

c.800 .... Hops begin to find their way into beer

1040 .... Weihenstephan, the oldest surviving brewery in the world, is founded near Munich

c.1400 .... British brewers begin to use hops in beer

1516 .... The Reinheitsgebot, the German beer purity law, is proclaimed by Duke Wilhelm IV of Bavaria

1698 .... Shepherd Neame, the UK's oldest surviving brewery, is founded in Kent

c.1700 .... Porter begins to gain popularity in the UK

1784 .... The first steam engine is installed in a brewery, in London

1785 .... Joseph Bramah invents a form of beer engine/handpump, paving the way for changes to the way beer is dispensed

1794 .... The first issue of the *Morning Advertiser*, the publicans' newspaper is published

c.1800 .... The India pale ale trade gathers momentum

1810 .... The first Oktoberfest is held in Munich, celebrating the marriage of Crown Prince Ludwig of Bavaria and Princess Therese of Saxony

1817 .... Daniel Wheeler patents a new method of roasting malt that changes for ever the flavour of porter and stout

1821 .... Henry Ricketts develops a split mould for producing glass bottles, making bottling more attractive to brewers

1830 .... The Beerhouse Act comes into law in the UK, leading to a huge increase in pubs brewing and selling their own beer

1841 .... Anton Dreher creates the first amber coloured lager at his Vienna brewery, giving rise to the Vienna lager style

1842 .... Josef Groll produces the world's first golden lager in Pilsen, creating the pilsner style

1845 .... UK Excise Acts imposing a tax on glass are repealed, leading to cheaper and more common glassware for beer

1862 .... Louis Pasteur conducts the first tests of what will become known as pasteurization

1874 .... The Manx Beer Purity Law is passed

1876 .... Bass registers Britain's first trademark, the red triangle

1883 .... Emil Christian Hansen, a scientist at Carlsberg in Denmark, isolates and cultivates the first single, pure strain of yeast

1892 ....William Painter of Baltimore, USA, introduces the crown cork as a new way to seal bottles

1904 ....The first fully automatic bottle-making equipment goes into use at the Toledo Glass Company in the USA, making beer bottling cheap, quick and efficient

1920 ....Prohibition is introduced in the USA

1930 ....London brewer Watney's trials pasteurized, keg beer

1933 ....Prohibition ends in the USA

1935 ....New Jersey's Krueger brewery markets the first canned beer

1959 ....Canadian Carling Black Label entrepreneur Eddie Taylor establishes Northern (later United) Breweries and begins acquiring UK breweries, stimulating consolidation that results in the Big Six UK national brewers in the 1970s

1963 ....The Society for the Preservation of Beer from the Wood is founded, as the brewing industry widely adopts metal casks

1971 ....The Campaign for Real Ale (CAMRA) is founded

1974 ....The first edition of the *Good Beer Guide* is published

1976 ....New Albion, in Sonoma, California, opens; it is the first microbrewery in the US craft beer revolution

1977 ....The first Great British Beer Festival is held, at Alexandra Palace, London

1977 ....Michael Jackson publishes *The World Guide to Beer*, inspiring beer drinkers and brewers the world over

1982 ....The first Great American Beer Festival is held, in Boulder, Colorado

1988 ....The British Guild of Beer Writers is formed in London

1989 ....Lager becomes the most widely consumed type of beer in the UK, overtaking ale

1989 ....The UK Government's Beer Orders lead to a huge shake up in the brewing industry

1990 ....The guest beer law is introduced in the UK, allowing publicans of national brewers' pubs to sell a cask beer of their own choosing

2002 ....Progressive Beer Duty is introduced in the UK, ensuring small brewers pay less tax on beer production than big companies

2008 ....The world's biggest brewer is created with the merger of InBev (itself a merger of Interbrew of Belgium and AmBev of Brazil) and Anheuser-Busch of the USA

The Four Classic British Brew Pubs

When the first edition of the *Good Beer Guide* was published in 1974, the traditional home-brew house was, like real ale in general, on its last legs. Only four such establishments were known to still exist (there are now more than 100 brew pubs across the UK). These four 'classics' were:

The All Nations, Madeley, Shropshire**
The Blue Anchor, Helston, Cornwall*
The Olde Swan (Ma Pardoe's), Netherton, West Midlands**
The Three Tuns, Bishop's Castle, Shropshire**

*Still brewing.

**Brewing ceased for a while but has been revived.

The Top 20 Take-Home Beer Brands in the UK

	Brand	Supplier
1	Stella Artois	A-B InBev UK
2	Foster's	Heineken UK
3	Carling	Molson Coors UK
4	Carlsberg	Carlsberg UK
5	Budweiser	A-B InBev UK
6	Carlsberg Export	Carlsberg UK
7	Kronenbourg 1664	Heineken UK
8	Beck's	A-B InBev UK
9	John Smith's Extra Smooth	Heineken UK
10	Guinness Draught	Diageo GB
11	Tennent's	C&C Group
12	Peroni	Miller Brands
13	San Miguel	Carlsberg UK
14	Stella Artois 4%	A-B InBev UK
15	Grolsch	Molson Coors UK
16	Carlsberg Special Brew	Carlsberg UK
17	Corona Extra	Wells & Young's
18	Boddingtons Draught	A-B InBev UK
19	Heineken	Heineken UK
20	Old Speckled Hen	Greene King

Figures correct to October 2010. Source: Nielsen ScanTrack.

Beer Heroes: Michael Jackson (1942–2007)

By common consent, no one has done more to open up the world of beer than writer Michael Jackson. Through his pioneering works *The World Guide to Beer*, *The Beer Companion*, *The Great Beers of Belgium* and the TV series *The Beer Hunter*, Michael placed beer firmly on the world map of gastronomic delights. He urged people – drinkers, brewers, publicans, restaurateurs and more – to treat beer with the respect it deserves. He led the way, blazing the trail into uncharted corners of the world, discovering beer styles that the rest of the planet had never encountered. He inspired so many of us to be more adventurous in our choice of tipple and, even more significantly, encouraged others to start brewing themselves. It is no coincidence that the craft brewing movement in the USA really began to grow at the same time as Michael's *World Guide to Beer* was first published there. The beer world lost Michael in 2007, but his influence will continue for years to come.

Celebrity Beers

All the following 'names' have connections with British beers.

Celebrity	Claim to Fame	Beer Connection
Alex Brodie	BBC journalist	Owner of Hawkshead Brewery
Tony Hadley	Pop singer	Partner in Red Rat brewery
Mark Hix	Chef	Own beer brewed by Palmers
Neil Morrissey	Actor	Partner in Morrissey Fox brewery
Prince Charles	Heir to throne	Owner of Duchy Originals brands
Jody Scheckter	Racing driver	Owner of Laverstoke Park brands
Rick Stein	Chef	Own beers brewed by Sharp's
Brian Turner	Chef	Own beer brewed by Thornbridge
Marco Pierre White	Chef	Own beer brewed by Lees

Fry's the Man

In a poll conducted by CAMRA for the Great British Beer Festival 2011, real ale fans overwhelmingly decided that the person they would most like to enjoy a pint with was comedian/actor/raconteur Stephen Fry.

CAMRA's National Chairmen

1972–3	Michael Hardman	**1983–5**	Tony Millns
1974	Chris Hutt	**1986–8**	Jim Scanlon
1975	Gordon Massey	**1989**	Rob Walker
1976	Chris Holmes	**1990–8**	John Cryne
1977	Chris Bruton	**1999–2003**	Dave Goodwin
1978	James Lynch	**2004–10**	Paula Waters
1979–80	Joe Goodwin	**2010–**	Colin Valentine
1981–2	Tim Amsden		

Dates are based on the Annual General Meetings the position holders chaired.

Beers Named After Pop Songs and Album Titles

The Triple fff brewery, based in Hampshire, specializes in naming beers after rock songs and album titles, but other breweries share the practice.

Beer (Brewery)	Artist
Apache Rose Peacock (Triple fff)	Red Hot Chili Peppers
Because the Night (Kelham Island)	Patti Smith Group
Black Night (Ridgeside)	Deep Purple
Comfortably Numb (Triple fff)	Pink Floyd
Dark Side of the Moon (Spire)	Pink Floyd
Dazed & Confused (Triple fff)	Led Zeppelin
Golden Brown (Butts)	Stranglers
How to Disappear Completely (BrewDog)	Radiohead
Moondance (Triple fff)	Van Morrison
Oh Boy (Bryncelyn)	Crickets
Pressed Rat and Warthog (Triple fff)	Cream
Rave On (Bryncelyn)	Buddy Holly
Rock Lobster (Triple fff)	B52s
Stairway to Heaven (Burton Bridge)	Led Zeppelin
Stormbringer (Abbeydale)	Deep Purple
Stormwatch (Cox & Holbrook)	Jethro Tull
Waterloo Sunset (Boggart)	Kinks
Whiter Shade of Pale (Spire)	Procul Harem
Winter Wonderland (Spire)	Johnny Mathis
Witches Promise (Triple fff)	Jethro Tull

Beer's Patron Saints

Beer enjoys the patronage of numerous saints, some only because of rather limited associations with beer and brewers, but others because they were said to have performed miracles and other feats involving beer. Listed below are the most prominent and their beery connections.

Saint	Lifespan	Feast Day
St Arnold/Arnulf of Metz	580–640	18 July

Bishop of Metz whose funeral pallbearers were refreshed by a bottomless mug of beer.

St Arnold/Arnulf of Soissons	1040–1087	14 August

Bishop of Soissons who advised his flock to drink beer rather than water, as it was safer.

St Augustine of Hippo	354–430	28 August

Bishop of Hippo (Algeria) who formerly enjoyed a hedonistic lifestyle, including copious beer drinking.

St Brigid/Bridget of Ireland	453–523	1 February

Pious chieftain's daughter (possibly) who turned her bathwater into beer to serve a visiting cleric.

St Columbanus	543–615	21 November

Irish itinerant missionary who multiplied bread and beer to feed his followers.

St Hildegarde of Bingen	1098–1179	17 September

Benedictine abbess and polymath who promoted the use of hops in beer.

St Lawrence	?–258	10 August

Papal deacon roasted alive by anti-Christian Emperor Valerian; brewers sought his patronage because they also often suffered fiery deaths in ancient times.

St Veronus	?–863	31 January

Miracle worker adopted by the lambic brewers of the Payottenland region, near Brussels, Belgium.

Ten Outstanding London Pubs and Bars

Des de Moor is author of *The CAMRA Guide to London's Best Beer Pubs & Bars*. Here he selects ten outstanding London outlets (listed solely alphabetically), on the basis of the range and quality of the draught (both cask ales and imported craft beers) and bottled beers they serve.

1 **Cask**, 6 Charlwood Street, SW1V 2EE
   Former estate pub transformed into a beer hunter's dream by well-informed owners, with ten unusual cask ales and a dazzling range of international bottles and craft kegs. Special tastings and Meet the Brewer events.

2 **Craft Beer Co**, 82 Leather Lane, EC1N 7TR
   An instant must visit when opened in June 2011, with 15 cask ales, 21 imported and domestic craft keg lines, and 300 bottles with numerous rarities and exclusives – and all in a proper old Victorian pub with a spectacular mirrored ceiling.

3 **The Crosse Keys**, 9 Gracechurch Street, EC3V 0DR
   Wetherspoon beer flagship with up to 25 cask ales among the spectacular pillars, staircases and sculptures of the former HSBC banking headquarters in the heart of the City.

4 **Euston Tap**, West Lodge, 190 Euston Road, NW1 2EF
   A Tardis of rare delights in one of the former lodges of Euston's demolished Doric Arch, with eight cask ales, 19 specialist kegs and over 100 bottles. Watch out for the precarious staircase.

5 **The Harp**, 47 Chandos Place, WC2N 4HS
   CAMRA's National Pub of the Year in 2011, with eight top local cask ales, legendary sausages and a warm welcome within a stone's throw of Trafalgar Square. The West End almost doesn't deserve such a great pub.

6 **King William IV**, 816 High Road, E10 6AE
   Worth the trip to Leyton for Brodie's rambling brew pub with up to 20 often eccentric beers on tap, even more in bottle, and a collection of junk worthy of Steptoe and Son.

7 **The Market Porter**, 9 Stoney Street, SE1 9AA
The historic core of what is now London's craft beer quarter around Borough Market, with 12 handpumps offering new and unusual cask delights. Opens early for the market, and often heaving.

8 **The Rake**, 14 Winchester Walk, SE1 9AG
London's international beer geek drop-in centre on the edge of Borough Market, with three cask beers, numerous imported kegs and 130 bottles, including serious rarities. Tiny, but an attractive wooden terrace provides spreading room.

9 **The Southampton Arms**, 139 Highgate Road, NW5 1LE
Transformed from a dodgy and decaying boozer into an outstanding contemporary ale and cider house, this place prides itself on only stocking products from small independent producers. Ten local and unusual cask ales and classic jazz vinyl.

10 **The White Horse**, 1 Parson's Green, SW6 4UL
Longstanding and rather posh specialist beer champion with eight top cask ales and a world beer list of more than 100, including plenty of strong and special choices. Still holding its own amongst growing competition.

Back Through the Baltic

In 2011, a group of British brewers and other enthusiasts set about re-creating the formidable journey once regularly made by stout from Britain to Russia. Back in the late 1700s, strong stouts became very popular in the court of the Russian tsar, so becoming known as imperial Russian stouts, but, to reach the royal household and other appreciative drinkers, the beers were forced to undergo a rough maritime crossing – over the choppy North Sea and on across the icy Baltic. For a voyage conceived by brewer Tim O'Rourke, the 21st-century crew boarded the 60-ft clipper *Thermopylae* at Greenwich in May 2011 and set sail for St Petersburg, calling at Copenhagen, Helsinki and other ports for en route celebrations of the imperial stout style. The beers they carried along with them – strong stouts and porters from numerous British breweries – were pronounced a success on their arrival in Russia a month later.

Unusual British Pub Names

Pub	Location
Angel & Greyhound	Oxford
Baltic Fleet	Liverpool, Merseyside
Bears Paw	High Legh, Cheshire
Bees in the Wall	Whittlesford, Cambridgeshire
Bell & Jorrocks	Frittenden, Kent
Belted Will	Hallbankgate, Cumbria
Blazing Donkey	Ramsgate, Kent
Blue Lias	Stockton, Warwickshire
Bree Louise	Euston, London
Briton's Protection	Manchester
Bucket of Blood	Phillack, Cornwall
Bull & Spectacles	Blithbury, Staffordshire
Bush, Blackbird & Thrush	East Peckham, Kent
Cape of Good Hope	Warwick
Carts Bog Inn	Langley, Northumberland
Case is Altered	Five Ways, Warwickshire
Cat & Custard Pot	Paddlesworth, Kent
Chemic Tavern	Leeds, West Yorkshire
Chip Shop Inn	Chip Shop, Devon
Coal Exchange	Emsworth, Hampshire
Cow & Snuffers	Cardiff
Cracke	Liverpool, Merseyside
Crown & Kettle	Manchester
Crown Posada	Newcastle-upon-Tyne, Tyne & Wear
Dog & Bell	Deptford, London
Donkey & Buskins	Layer-de-la-Haye, Essex
Drunken Duck	Barngates, Cumbria
Elephant's Nest Inn	Horndon, Devon
Flat Iron	Salford, Greater Manchester
Floods Tavern	St Ives, Cambridgeshire
Four Topped Oak	Widnes, Cheshire
Gate Hangs Well	Carlton, Leicestershire
Goblin Ha' Hotel	Gifford, East Lothian
Green Man & Black's Head Royal Hotel	Ashbourne, Derbyshire
Gribble Inn	Oving, West Sussex

Hark to Mopsey	Normanton, West Yorkshire
Hat & Beaver	Leicester
Hazel Pear Inn	Acton Bridge, Cheshire
Hoy & Helmet	South Benfleet, Essex
Jabez Clegg	Manchester
Jolly Taxpayer	Portsmouth, Hampshire
Kangaroo	Aston on Clun, Shropshire
Kicking Cuddy	Coxhoe, County Durham
Lad in the Lane	Erdington, Birmingham
Land of Liberty, Peace & Plenty	Heronsgate, Hertfordshire
Laughing Fish	Isfield, East Sussex
Leg of Mutton and Cauliflower	Ashtead, Surrey
Mad Cat	Pidley, Cambridgeshire
Morris Clown	Bampton, Oxfordshire
Old Dungeon Ghyll	Great Langdale, Cumbria
Old Thirteenth Cheshire Astley Volunteer Rifleman Corps Inn	Stalybridge, Greater Manchester
Only Running Footman	Mayfair, London
Periscope	Barrow-in-Furness, Cumbria
Peveril of the Peak	Manchester
Pink & Lily	Lacey Green, Buckinghamshire
Pipe and Gannex	Knowsley, Merseyside
Pyrotechnists Arms	Nunhead, London
Railway & Naturalist	Prestwich, Greater Manchester
Road to Morocco	Northampton
Queen Dowager	Teddington, London
Queen in the West	Lincoln
Quiet Woman	Earl Sterndale, Derbyshire
Royal Standard of England	Forty Green, Buckinghamshire
Sir Loin of Beef	Portsmouth, Hampshire
Smoking Dog	Malmesbury, Wiltshire
Strawbury Duck	Entwistle, Lancashire
Swan & Cemetery	Bury, Greater Manchester
Swan & Railway	Wigan, Greater Manchester
Three Legs of Man	Manchester
Tucker's Grave	Faulkland, Somerset
Virgins & Castle	Kenilworth, Warwickshire
Volunteer Canteen	Liverpool, Merseyside
Young Vanish	Glapwell, Derbyshire

Coin-op Beer

In 1981, just when cask beer seemed to be making a comeback in the UK, Middlesex company Grundy launched new keg beer dispensing equipment for use in pubs. Under the headline 'When your customers are fighting for counter space, use the wall', the Teddington-based firm advertised details of its coin-operated, self-service, draught bitter or lager vending machine. There was, of course, a flaw in the thankfully short-lived system. What if you wanted a bag of nuts or crisps as well?

London Brewers Alliance

'The Alliance hopes to unite those who make local beer with those that love it, and represent the vibrant heritage and contemporary scene of beer brewing in the great city of London', so reads the mission statement of the London Brewers Alliance, founded in 2010. Fourteen brewers, both large and small, are currently members of the association.

Brew Wharf	Meantime
Brodie's	Redemption
Camden Town	Sambrook's
The Florence	Twickenham
Fuller's	Windsor & Eton
Ha'Penny	Young's*
Kernel	Zerodegrees

*Brewing as Wells & Young's in Bedford.

The Landlord's Tie

Al Murray's comic creation the Pub Landlord has been feted by viewers and critics alike, but one of the first organizations to recognize his talent – and his flair for extracting humour from the world of beer and pubs – was the British Guild of Beer Writers. The beer scribes awarded Murray the Maurice Lovett Award for Humour at its annual awards evening in 1996. Ever since, the Pub Landlord has sported a Guild tie. Look for the 'quill-and-tankard' logo beneath the dark- and royal-blue stripes.

Traditional Cask Sizes

Butt	108 gallons (no longer used)
Puncheon	72 gallons (no longer used)
Hogshead	54 gallons (now rarely used)
Barrel	36 gallons
Half Hogshead	27 gallons (now rarely used)
Kilderkin or Kil/Kiln	18 gallons
Anker	10 gallons (now rarely used)
Firkin	9 gallons
Pin	$4^{1}/_{2}$ gallons

Party Poopers

As Christmas party tricks go, it seems like fun, but New South Wales policeman Andrew Lawrance paid the price in 2008 when his employers saw red over his particular secret skill. To entertain the crowd, Sgt Lawrance decided to demonstrate his ability to open bottles of beer with his penis, attaching an opener to the piercing on his member. Sadly, the powers that be declared this to be inappropriate behaviour for a member of the force and Lawrance was dismissed from his job.

The World's Top Beer-Producing Countries

	Country	Million Hl		Country	Million Hl
1	China	410.3	11	Ukraine	32.0
2	USA	230.1	12	South Africa	27.6
3	Russian Federation	114.0	13	Netherlands	26.5
4	Brazil	106.3	14	Venezuela	24.9
5	Germany	100.6	15	Canada	23.7
6	Mexico	82.3	16	Romania	20.8
7	Japan	61.3	17	Czech Republic	19.8
8	UK	49.5	18	Colombia	19.0
9	Poland	35.6	19	South Korea	18.6
10	Spain	33.4	20	Belgium & Luxembourg	18.0

Figures given are for 2008. Source: British Beer & Pub Association Statistical Handbook 2010.

British Beer and Pub Association Members

The British Beer and Pub Association (BBPA) is a trade organization representing businesses that account for around 98% of all beer brewed in the UK and who own more than half of the country's 54,000 pubs.

3M Healthcare
Admiral Taverns Ltd
Adnams plc
Alectica Ltd
Anheuser-Busch InBev
Arkell's Brewery Ltd
Barracuda Group
Black Sheep Brewery plc
Brakspear Pub Company
C and C Group plc
Camerons Brewing Ltd
Carlsberg UK
Charles Wells Ltd
Close Brewery Rentals
Daleside Brewery
Daniel Batham & Son Ltd
Daniel Thwaites plc
Diageo plc
Elgood & Sons Ltd
Enterprise Inns plc
Everards Brewery Ltd
Felinfoel Brewery Co Ltd
Frederic Robinson Ltd
Fuller, Smith & Turner plc
George Bateman & Son Ltd
Gray & Sons (Chelmsford) Ltd
Hall & Woodhouse Ltd
Harvey & Son (Lewes) Ltd
Heavitree Brewery plc
Heineken UK
Heron & Brearley Ltd
Holden's Brewery Ltd

Hook Norton Brewery Co Ltd
Hydes Brewery Ltd
iNTERTAIN Ltd
JC & RH Palmer Ltd
JW Lees & Co (Brewers) Ltd
John Gaunt and Partners
Joseph Holt Ltd
Kurnia Licensing Consultants
Liberation Group
Maclay Group plc
Marston's plc
McMullen & Sons Ltd
Miller Brands UK
Mitchells & Butlers
Mitchells of Lancaster Ltd
Molson-Coors Ltd
Poppleston Allen
Punch Taverns
RW Randall
Robert Cain & Company Ltd
Route Organisation
SA Brain & Company Ltd
Sharp's Brewery
Shepherd Neame Ltd
St Austell Brewery Co. Ltd
T&R Theakston
Thomas Hardy Brewing & Packaging Ltd
Timothy Taylor & Co Ltd
Titanic Brewery
Wadworth & Co Ltd
Weston Castle
Young & Co's Brewery plc

Names of companies as listed by the BBPA in August 2011.

Beer That's Out of This World

In 2008, Japanese citizens were the first to savour beer that had extra-terrestrial origins. Space Barley (5.5% ABV) was created by Sapporo Breweries using barley that had been grown in a laboratory on the International Space Station. Just 100 litres of the beer were produced.

Beer Magazines and Newspapers

Ale Street News, USA	Bi-monthly	alestreetnews.com
All About Beer, USA	Bi-monthly	allaboutbeer.com
Beer & Brewer Magazine, Australia/New Zealand	5 issues/year	beerandbrewer.com
Beer Advocate, USA	Monthly	beeradvocate.com/mag
Beer Connoisseur, USA	Quarterly	beerconnoisseur.com
Beer, UK	Quarterly	camra.org.uk
Bier!, Netherlands	Quarterly	birdypublishing.nl
Brewers' Guardian, UK	Bi-monthly	brewersguardian.com
Brewery History, UK	Quarterly	breweryhistory.com/journal
Celebrator Beer News, USA	Bi-monthly	celebrator.com
Draft Magazine, USA	Bi-monthly	draftmag.com
Il Mondo della Birra, Italy	Monthly	ilmondodellabirra.it
The New Brewer, USA	Bi-monthly	brewersassociation.org
Taps, The Beer Magazine, Canada	Quarterly	tapsmagazine.com
What's Brewing, UK	Monthly	camra.org.uk*
Zymurgy, USA	Bi-monthly	brewersassociation.org*

*Membership publications for the relevant organizations.

Two States Still Say No

Although home-brewing was federally legalized by President Jimmy Carter in 1978, there remain two American states in which it is illegal to brew beer at home. Following positive law changes in Utah in 2009 and Oklahoma in 2010, now only Alabama and Mississippi still ban home beer production, despite major campaigns to change the status quo.

Beer City USA

Since 2009, US craft beer guru Charlie Papazian, in his role as Beer Examiner for Examiner.com, has organized an annual poll to discover what drinkers consider to be the best beer city in the USA. Anyone can vote and the first winners (joint) were Asheville (North Carolina) and Portland (Oregon). A year later, Asheville – a small hill town of some 80,000 people that is home to eight breweries – ran out the clear winner and repeated its triumph in 2011, as the table of results below reveals.

	City	Votes	%
1	Asheville, North Carolina	7,002	46.68%
2	San Diego, California	2,374	15.83%
3	Portland, Oregon	1,495	9.97%
4	Bend, Oregon	821	5.47%
5	St Louis, Missouri	549	3.66%
6	Milwaukee, Wisconsin	391	2.61%
7	Philadelphia, Pennsylvania	366	2.44%
8	Seattle, Washington	336	2.24%
9	San Francisco/Oakland-Bay Area, California	320	2.13%
10	Chicago, Illinois	287	1.91%

Source: Examiner.com.

Some Important International Trade Fairs

Fair	Location	Month
Brau Beviale	Nuremberg, Germany	November
Cellar to Seller	Birmingham, UK	April
China Brew	Beijing, China	September
Craft Brewers Conference/ BrewExpo America	Varies, USA	March
NBWA* Convention & Trade Show	Las Vegas, USA	September
Pianeta Birra	Rimini, Italy	February
Pivovar	Moscow, Russia	April
SIBA** Annual Brewing Conference	Stratford-upon-Avon, UK	April

*National Beer Wholesalers Association. **Society of Independent Brewers.

Floor Maltings in the UK

The method of converting barley into malt has changed considerably with advances in technology. There are, however, still four surviving traditional floor maltings in the UK, where soaked barley is spread over a large stone floor area to germinate and then turned regularly by hand.

Maltings	Location
Crisp	Great Ryburgh, Norfolk
Fawcett's	Castleford, West Yorkshire
Tuckers	Newton Abbot, Devon
Warminster	Wiltshire

Imperial/US and Metric Conversion Formulae

From	To	Multiply by
imperial pints	litres	0.5683
US pints	litres	0.4732
imperial gallons	litres	4.5461
US gallons	litres	3.7854
imperial gallons	hectolitres	0.0455
US gallons	hectolitres	0.0379
36-gallon barrels	hectolitres	1.6366
US 31-gallon barrels	hectolitres	1.1735

From	To	Multiply by
litres	imperial pints	1.7597
litres	US pints	2.1134
litres	imperial gallons	0.22
litres	US gallons	0.2642
hectolitres	imperial gallons	21.997
hectolitres	US gallons	26.4217
hectolitres	36-gallon barrels	0.611
hectolitres	US 31-gallon barrels	0.8523

From	To	Multiply by
imperial pints/gallons	US pints/gallons	1.2001
US pints/gallons	imperial pints/gallons	0.8327

The Top Five Individual American Brewpubs

	Brewery (State)	US Barrels*
1	Hopworks Urban Brewery (Oregon)	6,364
2	Boundary Bay Brewing Co (Oregon)	6,187
3	Laurelwood Brewing Co (Oregon)	5,952
4	Cascade Brewery/Raccoon Lodge & Brewpub (Washington)	5,652
5	Elysian Brewing Co (Washington)	5,500

*Annual output. Brewery restaurants with at least 25 per cent of beer sales on site.

Figures given are for 2010. Source: Brewers Association.

Head Brewers of Major British Breweries

Adnams	Fergus Fitzgerald
Arkell's	Don Bracher
Badger	Toby Heasman
Banks's	Richard Frost
Batemans	Martin Cullimore
Batham's	Martin Birch
Belhaven	George Howell
Black Sheep	Alan Dunn
Brains	Bill Dobson
Caledonian	Ian Kennedy
Camerons	Martin Dutoy
Coors (Burton)	Andrew Robinson
Copper Dragon	Gordon Wilkinson
Donnington	James Arkell
Elgood's	Alan Pateman
Everards	Graham Giblett
Felinfoel	John Reed
Fuller's	John Keeling
Greene King	John Bexon
Harveys	Miles Jenner
Holden's	Roger Bennett
Holt's	Keith Sheard
Hook Norton	James Clarke
Hop Back	Steve Wright
Hydes	Paul Jeffries
Jennings	Jeremy Pettman
Lees	Michael Lees-Jones
McMullen	Chris Evans
Marston's	Emma Gilleland
Meantime	Alastair Hook
Palmers	Darren Batten
Randalls	Matt Polli
Ringwood	Jeff Drew
Robinson's	Martyn Weeks
St Austell	Roger Ryman
Sharp's	Stuart Howe
Shepherd Neame	David Holmes
Taylor	Peter Eells
Thwaites	Steve Fielding
Wadworth	Brian Yorston
Wells & Young's	Jim Robertson
William Worthington	Jim Appelbee
Wychwood	Jeff Drew

Details correct as of August 2011.

Major Beer Festivals Worldwide

Location	Festival	Month
Belgium		
Leuven	Zythos Beer Fest	April
Eizeringen	Day of the Kriek	June
Brussels	Belgian Beer Weekend	September
Hasselt	Weekend der Belgische Bieren	November
Essen	Kerstbierfestival	December
Canada		
Montreal	Mondial de la Bière	June
Victoria	Great Canadian Beer Festival	September
Denmark		
Copenhagen	Copenhagen Beer Festival	May
France		
Strasbourg	Mondial de la Bière	October
Germany		
Munich	Oktoberfest	September
Netherlands		
Oisterwijk	Biermatinee	July
Amsterdam	Pint Bokbierfestival	October
New Zealand		
Wellington	Beervana	August
Sweden		
Stockholm	Stockholm Beer and Whisky Festival	October
UK		
Varies	National Winter Ales Festival	January
London	London Drinker	March
Cambridge	Cambridge Beer Festival	May
Cardiff	Great Welsh Beer & Cider Festival	June
Edinburgh	Scottish Real Ale Festival	June
London	Great British Beer Festival	August
Peterborough	Peterborough Beer Festival	August
USA		
Portland, Oregon	Spring Beer & Wine Festival	April
Somerville, Massachusetts	New England Real Ale Exhibition (NERAX)	April
Denver	Great American Beer Festival	September

Some Technical Brewing Terms

Adjunct	A cereal other than barley used in beer
Aeration	Allowing oxygen into the wort to aid fermentation
Alpha acid	Acid in hops that provides bitterness
Attenuation	The degree to which wort is fermented
Autolysis	The breakdown of yeast in aged beer, giving umami flavours
Bottom-fermenting	Yeast mostly sits at the bottom of the wort while fermenting (lager)
Bright beer	Beer that has been filtered or fined, leaving no yeast in suspension
Burtonization	Adding salts to liquor to replicate the water of Burton-on-Trent
Chill proof	Clarifying beer to remove solids that would cause haze at low temperatures
Cold break	Rapid cooling of wort to remove proteins and other material
Condition	The amount of dissolved carbon dioxide in a beer
Conditioning	Maturing beer in tanks or bottles to improve flavours and carbonation
Decoction	European method of mashing, involving more than one mash vessel and varying temperatures
Dry hopping	Adding unboiled hops to a beer during or after fermentation to enhance aroma
Esters	Fruit- or solvent-flavoured organic compounds created during fermentation
Ethanol	Alcohol created by fermentation; also known as ethyl alcohol
Extract	The amount of sugar in the wort
Fermentation	The conversion by yeast of sugars into alcohol and carbon dioxide
Finings	Substances used to clarify beer
First runnings	The wort run off from the mash tun before sparging or the addition of fresh liquor to extract more sugar from the grains
Flocculation	The natural clumping together of yeast cells
Grist	The mix of malt and other cereals that, with liquor, forms the mash

Gyle	A batch of beer
Hot break	Boiling of wort to remove proteins and other material
Infusion	Mashing process involving soaking grains in hot liquor
Isinglass	Finings made from the swim bladder of a tropical fish
Isomerization	The conversion of hop components during the boil to enhance the bitterness and increase solubility
Kräusening	Adding young fermenting wort to beer to encourage new fermentation
Lagering	Cold maturation for long periods
Liquor	Brewing water
Mash	The mix of grains and hot liquor that starts the brewing process
Milling	Crushing the grains prior to mashing
Original gravity	A measure of the specific gravity prior to fermentation
Parti-gyle	Brewing beers of varying strengths from one mash
Pasteurization	Heat treating beer to kill off yeast cells and bacteria
pH	The level of acidity in liquor or in a mash
Pitching	Adding yeast to a brew to start fermentation
Priming	Adding new sugars to a beer during packaging to encourage new fermentation
Racking	Transferring beer into casks or kegs
Saccharification	The conversion of starches in malt into sugars
Sparging	Spraying mashed grains with hot water to gain more extract
Specific gravity	The density of a liquid compared with water; indicates the amount of fermentable material
Strike heat	The starting temperature of the mash
Top-fermenting	Yeast mostly sits on the top of the wort while fermenting (ale)
Trub	Proteins, yeast and other solid matter extracted during brewing
Ullage	Waste beer; also the space allowed above beer in a container
Wort	The unfermented sweet, sugary liquid produced by the mash

Beers' Dates of Birth

The following list reveals when some famous beers were first brewed.

Adnams Broadside	1972	Innis & Gunn Oak Aged Beer	2003
Alaskan Smoked Porter	1988	Jenlain Ambrée	1922
Anchor Liberty Ale	1975	Manns Brown Ale	1902
Batemans Victory Ale	1987	Marston's Old Empire	2003
Brains SA Gold	2006	Meantime India Pale Ale	2005
Brooklyn Lager	1988	Morland Old Speckled Hen	1979
Budweiser	1876	Pilsner Urquell	1842
Budweiser Budvar	1895	Robinson's Old Tom	1899
Caledonian Deuchars IPA	1991	St Austell Tribute	1999
Carlsberg Special Brew	1950	Samuel Adams Boston Lager	1985
Eggenberg Samichlaus	1979	Schneider Aventinus	1907
Exmoor Gold	1986	Schneider Weisse	1872
Fuller's ESB	1971	Shepherd Neame Spitfire	1990
Fuller's London Pride	1959	Sierra Nevada Pale Ale	1980
Fuller's Vintage Ale	1997	Stella Artois	1926
Gale's HSB	1959	Taylor Landlord	1953
Harveys Armada Ale	1988	Wadworth 6X	1921
Hoegaarden	1966	Westmalle Dubbel	1926
Hook Norton Old Hooky	1977	Westmalle Tripel	1934
Hop Back Summer Lightning	1988	Young's Double Chocolate Stout	1997

The Temple of a Million Bottles

Buddhist monks in Thailand have created a whole complex of religious buildings using old beer bottles. Their favoured brands are Heineken (green bottles) and Chang (brown) and the bottles, built into a concrete core, are said to be easy to clean and offer good light. The monks began collecting the bottles in 1984 and, with the help of local authorities, have amassed enough to build a temple, prayer rooms, a crematorium, living quarters and a hall at their Wat Pa Maha Chedi Kaew base in Sisaket province, close to the border with Cambodia. Recycled bottle caps are also employed to make mosaics of Buddha in the temple, contributing to the site's increasing importance as a tourist attraction.

The Worst Brewery in Literature?

Anthony Trollope's 1863 novel *Rachel Ray* focuses on one Luke Rowan, a young legal clerk who inherits a share in a failing Devon brewery. Bungall and Tappitt doesn't sound a very grand concern and, sadly, its output fits the name. The author sums up the quality of the beer thus:

'It was a sour and muddy stream that flowed from their vats: a beverage disagreeable to the palate, and very cold and uncomfortable to the stomach'

The LOBI Group

Reflecting the increasing presence of quality lager production in the UK (a country unfortunately long known for its shoddy attempts at this grand European brewing technique), LOBI was established in 2009. Its initials standing for Lager Of the British Isles, this is an association that promotes beers that a) have a genuine lagering period, with decent maturation times; b) are produced at volumes that don't affect their hand-crafted nature; and c) use only high quality ingredients, including a lager yeast, and not cheap adjuncts (particularly no rice or maize). Membership encompasses lager brewers of integrity up and down the country, as listed below, all of them committed to the above principles.

Cotswold	Mitchell Krause
Freedom	Randalls
Harviestoun	WEST
Hepworth	

Who Was JD Wetherspoon?

Established in 1979, JD Wetherspoon is one of the UK's largest pub companies, with more than 800 outlets. The name of the group comes from two sources. The 'JD' element is borrowed from the TV series *The Dukes of Hazzard*, which was popular at the time the first pub was opened, with JD (Jefferson Davis aka 'Boss') Hogg, the Dukes' adversary. The Wetherspoon part comes from the surname of a teacher that company founder Tim Martin knew while growing up in New Zealand.

Five Facts About Hops

The Latin name for the hop is *humulus lupulus*, the second word meaning 'wolf-like', after the way Romans noticed the plant ran wild 'like a wolf among sheep'.

The hop is a member of the hemp family and a relative of both cannabis and the stinging nettle.

Hops can grow to 16 feet or more once strung along a serious of poles in a hop garden. Hop roots, meanwhile, can burrow as deep as 12 feet.

Male and female hops grow as separate plants, but only female hops are used in brewing.

As well as providing bitterness and other flavours, hops act as a natural preservative, keeping beer fresh.

Beer Football Sponsorship

Here are some of the major breweries and brands that have sponsored teams in the English and Scottish football leagues in the recent past.

Brewery/Brand	Team
Banks's	Walsall
Carlsberg	Liverpool
	Wimbledon
Chang	Everton
Carling	Celtic
	Rangers
Greene King	Ipswich Town
	Mansfield Town
Guinness	Queen's Park Rangers
Holsten	Tottenham Hotspur
Labatt	Nottingham Forest
Lees	Oldham Athletic
Marston's	Derby County
	Wrexham
McEwan's Lager	
	Blackburn Rovers
	Newcastle United
	Rangers
Newcastle Brown	
	Newcastle United
Robinson's	Stockport County
St Austell	Exeter City
Shipstone's	Nottingham Forest
Tennent's	Celtic
	Preston North End
	Rangers
Wards	Sheffield United

The Party Bike

The Metrofiets cycle company in Portland, Oregon, has found a way of merging two of the city's greatest pastimes – drinking beer and cycling. The company hires out a specially designed party bike, an extraordinary vehicle fully equipped to make any party go with a swing. The bike houses two taps, space to install a keg of beer, a CO_2 dispense system, a drip tray, a serving counter and a stereo. Just don't drink and pedal!

Beer Makes You Fat? Wrong!

Contrary to widespread popular belief, beer is not excessively fattening. Compared to other drinks, including wine, spirits and even apple juice, beer has fewer calories. Of course, if you load up on crisps, peanuts and pork scratchings while supping your pub pint, and call in for a kebab on the way home, then weight control is always likely to be more difficult!

Drink	Calories/100 ml
Beer (4.6%)	41
Wine (12%)	77
Spirits	250
Milk	64
Orange juice	42
Apple juice	47

Source: British Beer & Pub Association.

Becoming a Beer Judge

There are lots of competitions in which you need no qualifications to judge beer but there are good schemes that aim to furnish you with the knowledge, experience and certification that may open even more doors. In the USA, the highly regarded Beer Judge Certification Program (BJCP) has been running since 1985. It offers style guidelines for beers and sets examinations, allowing participants to progress up its ranks with knowledge gained. The BJCP's activities are now spreading around the world, as interest in becoming a beer judge increases. In the UK, The Beer Academy launched its own How to Judge Beer programme in 2011.

Common Brewing and Pub Abbreviations

ABV ....Alcohol by Volume
ABW ....Alcohol by Weight
AHA...American Homebrewers Association
ALMR .... Association of Licensed Multiple Retailers
BA.. Brewers Association
BBPA.. British Beer & Pub Association
BFBi............Brewing, Food & Beverage Industry Suppliers' Association
BII...British Institute of Innkeeping
BJCP ....Beer Judge Certification Program
BRI... Brewing Research International
CAMRA ....Campaign for Real Ale
CBOB .... Champion Beer of Britain
DAB..Dortmunder Actien Brauerei
EBC ....European Brewery Convention
EBCU.. European Beer Consumers Union
EKG .... East Kent Goldings (hop)
ESB ....Extra Special Bitter
FV .... Fermentation Vessel
GBBF...Great British Beer Festival
GBG.. Good Beer Guide
HLT.. Hot Liquor Tank
IBD ....Institute of Brewing & Distilling
IFBB...Independent Family Brewers of Britain
IPA...India Pale Ale
LOBI .... Lager Of the British Isles
LVA...Licensed Victuallers' Association
MT .... Mash Tun
NHA ....National Hop Association
OG .... Original Gravity
PA...Pale Ale
PBD .... Progressive Beer Duty
PET.......................................Polyethylene Terephthalate (plastic bottle)
S&N...Scottish & Newcastle
SIBA ....Society of Independent Brewers
SPBW ....Society for the Preservation of Beer from the Wood
WGV .... Whitbread Golding Variety (hop)
WSTA..Wine and Spirit Trade Association

The Price of Fame

*'Were I in an ale-house in London! I would give all
my fame for a pot of ale and safety.'*

Henry V, Act 3, Scene 2, William Shakespeare

Lambic Beers

The spontaneously-fermented beers of Belgium are noted for their 'funky', earthy, rustic and often tart flavours. They are created when wort is subjected to wild yeasts in the atmosphere and then fermented/matured for months, if not years, in wooden casks that are riddled with benign, character-building bacteria. However, the final product tends to be packaged and presented in four quite different ways, as outlined below.

Plain lambic	A still, sour, draught drink blended from various casks
Faro	A diluted and sweetened form of plain lambic (no longer common)
Gueuze	A sparkling bottled drink, a mix of young and old lambic
Fruit lambic	A sparkling bottled drink, laced and fermented with cherries (kriek), raspberries (framboise/frambozen) or other fruits

The National Brewing Library

Britain's National Brewing Library is housed at Oxford Brookes University in Headington, Oxford. The impressive English-language archive is largely comprised of books permanently loaned by the Institute of Brewing & Distilling and back-copies of brewing journals, but also included are company publications and numerous scientific texts. A separate collection is dedicated to books donated by the estate of the late Michael Jackson. It includes some 1,500 titles Michael acquired during his career as a beer writer, plus copies of his own works, along with notebooks and other information gathered over 40 years of beer writing. Researchers are advised to make an appointment to visit.

Towns and Cities With Own Native Beer Styles

Town/City	Beer Style
Bamberg	Rauchbier
Berlin	Berliner Weisse
Budweis (České Budějovice)	Budweiser
Burton-upon-Trent	Pale ale
Cologne	Kölsch
Dortmund	Export
Düsseldorf	Alt
Einbeck	Bock
Hoegaarden	Witbier
London	Porter
Munich	Märzen
Newcastle-upon-Tyne	Strong brown ale
Oudenaarde	Old brown ale
Pilsen	Pilsner
San Francisco	Steam beer
Vienna	Vienna red

The Prince in Exile

Prince Luitpold of Bavaria may no longer have ceremonial duties following the abolition of the state's monarchy after World War I, but he's still an important figure in southern Germany, especially in brewing circles. Luitpold runs Kaltenberg brewery, based in two locations, including a fairy-tale castle, about 30 miles west of Munich. Because of its location outside the city, however, Kaltenberg is not allowed to take part in Munich's famous Oktoberfest, an issue that jars somewhat when several of the participating breweries are now owned by multi-national companies. The Prince is also aggrieved by the fact that it was the wedding of his own great-great grandfather, King Ludwig I, that inspired the Oktoberfest celebration in the first place. As a response to this enforced exile, Luitpold has set up his own outdoor extravaganza. Held every July in the extensive grounds of his castle brewery, the Ritterturnier is a spectacular medieval jousting tournament at which gallons of Kaltenberg beer, including a strong lager called Ritterbock, brewed specially for the occasion, are consumed by around 120,000 visitors.

An A–Z of 'Must Try' Beers

A	Amber Shock	Birrificio Italiano (Italy)
B	Black Albert	Struise (Belgium)
C	Celebrator	Ayinger (Germany)
D	Duchesse de Bourgogne	Verhaeghe (Belgium)
E	Espresso	Dark Star (UK)
F	Flekovsky Tmavy Lezak	U Fleků (Czech Republic)
G	Grottenbier	St Bernardus (Belgium)
H	Hitachino Nest White Ale	Kiuchi (Japan)
I	It's Alive!	Mikkeler (Denmark)
J	Jenlain Ambrée	Duyck (France)
K	Kwak	Bosteels (Belgium)
L	Ligera	Birrificio Lambrate (Italy)
M	Matilda	Goose Island (USA)
N	Norwegian Wood	Handbryggeriet (Norway)
O	Oerbier	De Dolle (Belgium)
P	Pliny the Elder	Russian River (USA)
Q	Quadrupel	La Trappe (Netherlands)
R	Ripper	Green Jack (UK)
S	Sparkling Ale	Coopers (Australia)
T	Troublette	Caracole (Belgium)
U	Urbock 23°	Eggenberg (Austria)
V	Vitus	Weihenstephan (Germany)
W	World Wide Stout	Dogfish Head (USA)
X	XXXB	Batemans (UK)
Y	Yankee	Rooster's (UK)
Z	Zinnebir	De la Senne (Belgium)

List compiled from three 'must try' books: *300 Beers to Try Before You Die!* by Roger Protz, *1001 Beers You Must Try Before You Die* edited by Adrian Tierney-Jones, and *500 Beers* by Zak Avery.

Beer With No Name

By the 1970s, beer in the USA had descended to the level of basic commodity. Some manufacturers at the bottom of the downward spiral of quality were even turning out cheap cans that were sold simply as 'Beer', with no branding whatsoever, not even a supermarket own label.

Who Owns Whom

Ownership of beer brands by multinational companies has become more complicated than ever. Below is a list of some of the world's best known beer brands and the major companies that (currently) own them.

Brand	Owner	Brand	Owner
Achouffe	Duvel Moortgat	Dos Equis	Heineken
Adelscott	Heineken	Dreher (Hungary)	SABMiller
Affligem	Heineken	Dreher (Italy)	Heineken
Aldaris	Carlsberg	Duckstein	Carlsberg
Amstel	Heineken	Duvel	Duvel Moortgat
Ansells	Carlsberg	Edelweiss	Heineken
Baltika	Carlsberg	Faxe	Royal Unibrew
Bass	A-B InBev	Feldschlössen	Carlsberg
Beamish	Heineken	Fischer	Heineken
Beck's	A-B InBev	Flowers	A-B InBev
Belle-Vue	A-B InBev	Foster's	Foster's
Bintang	Heineken	Franziskaner	A-B InBev
Blue Moon	Molson Coors	Fürstenberg	Heineken
Boag's	Lion Nathan	Gambrinus	SABMiller
Boddingtons	A-B InBev	Giraf	Royal Unibrew
Bohemia	A-B InBev	Goose Island	A-B InBev
Boon	Palm*	Gösser	Heineken
Brahma	A-B InBev	Gouden Boom	Palm
Budweiser	A-B InBev	Grimbergen	Carlsberg
Caledonian	Heineken	Grolsch	SABMiller
Carling	Molson Coors	Guinness	Diageo
Carlsberg	Carlsberg	Hacker-Pschorr	Heineken
Castle	SABMiller	Hahn	Lion Nathan
Castlemaine XXXX	Lion Nathan	Hansa	SABMiller
Ceres	Royal Unibrew	Hapkin	Heineken
Ciney	Heineken	Harbin	A-B InBev
Cobra	Molson Coors	Harp	Diageo
Coors	Molson Coors	Heineken	Heineken
Corona	Grupo Modelo	Henninger	Carlsberg
Cruzcampo	Heineken	Hertog Jan	A-B InBev
De Koninck	Duvel Moortgat	Hoegaarden	A-B InBev
Desperados	Heineken	Holsten	Carlsberg
Diebels	A-B InBev	Hürlimann	Carlsberg

Jupiler	A-B InBev	Radegast	SABMiller
Kalnapilis	Royal Unibrew	Ringnes	Carlsberg
Kanterbräu	Carlsberg	Rodenbach	Palm
Kilkenny	Diageo	Rolling Rock	A-B InBev
Kozel	SABMiller	Sagres	Heineken
Kronenbourg	Carlsberg	St Pauli Girl	A-B InBev
Krusovice	Heineken	Sharp's	Molson Coors
Kulmbacher	Heineken	Skol	A-B InBev
Labatt's	A-B InBev	John Smith's	Heineken
Lapin Kulta	Heineken	Snow	SABMiller
Lech	SABMiller	Sol	Heineken
Leffe	A-B InBev	Spaten	A-B InBev
Leinenkugel's	SABMiller	Speight's	Lion Nathan
Liefmans	Duvel Moortgat	Starobrno	Heineken
Löwenbräu	A-B InBev	Staropramen	StarBev
M&B	Molson Coors	Steinlager	Lion Nathan
Mac's	Lion Nathan	Stella Artois	A-B InBev
Maes	Heineken	Stones	Molson Coors
Marathon	A-B InBev	Super Bock	Carlsberg
Michelob	A-B InBev	Svyturys	Carlsberg
Miller	SABMiller	Swan	Lion Nathan
Molson	Molson Coors	Synebrichoff	Carlsberg
Moretti	Heineken	Tatra	Heineken
Mort Subite	Heineken	Tecate	Heineken
Murphy's	Heineken	Tetley's	Carlsberg
Mythos	Carlsberg	Tiger	Heineken*
Newcastle Brown	Heineken	Toohey's	Lion Nathan
Okocim	Carlsberg	Tuborg	Carlsberg
Oranjeboom	A-B InBev	Tyskie	SABMiller
Palm	Palm	Utenos	Carlsberg
Paulaner	Heineken	Victoria Beer	Foster's
Pelforth	Heineken	Vratislav	StarBev
Peroni	SABMiller	Warka	Heineken
Piedboeuf	A-B InBev	Weinhard's	SABMiller
Pilsner Urquell	SABMiller	Wieckse Witte	Heineken
Poretti	Carlsberg	Worthington's	Molson Coors
Pripps	Carlsberg	Zipfer	Heineken
Quilmes	A-B InBev	Zywiec	Heineken

*Joint venture.

British Breweries in Unusual Locations

It's common to find new breweries setting up home in premises once occupied by other breweries, or taking over former dairies and barns, but here are some more unusual places occupied by British breweries.

Location	Brewery(ies)
Abattoir	Slaughterhouse
Airfield	Bartrams
Bakery	Great Western/St George's/Townes
Bird park	Paradise
Carpet factory	WEST
Chicken shed	Stonehouse
Cider mill	RCH
Coffin shop	Griffin Inn
Dockyard	Nelson
Dynamite store	Malvern Hills
Equestrian centre	Weetwood
Grocer's shop	Riverhead
Holiday park	Haywood Bad Ram/Plassey
Kennels	Prior's Well
Nuclear bunker	Lizard
Paint works	Derby
Polish works	Sheffield
Pork pie factory	Salamander
Porn cinema	Milk Street
Restaurant	Ramsgate
Saw mill	Purple Moose
School	Bewdley/Orkney
Sheep park	Country Life
Smoke house	Green Jack
Soft drinks factory	Jersey
Station	Richmond
Tennis pavilion	Bank Top
Textile mill	Millstone
Toilet	Gwynant/Malt B/Old Bog
Tram power station	Saltaire
Turkey shed	Little Valley
Vineyard	Felstar/Mersea Island/Old Luxters/Whittingtons

Beer by Numbers

Carlsberg-owned Baltika Breweries is based in St Petersburg, Russia, and operates the largest brewery in Europe. Unusually, its wide range of beers have numbered names. The style of each beer is shown below.

Number/Name	Style of Beer	ABV
0 Non-alcoholic Beer	Low alcohol	less than 0.5%
1 Light	Pale lager	4.4%*
2 Pale	Pale lager with rice	4.7%
3 Classic	Lager	4.8%
4 Original	Vienna lager/rye beer	5.6%
5 Golden	Lager	5.3%
6 Porter	Baltic porter	7%
7 Export	Dortmunder Export	5.4%
8 Wheat	Weizen	5%
9 Extra	Strong lager	8%

*No longer in production.

Burton Unions and Yorkshire Squares

There are two types of unusual fermentation systems native to the UK, and both are still in use today. The Burton unions can be found only at Marston's brewery in Burton-on-Trent. Used for brewing Pedigree Bitter, the unions are a series of linked wooden casks in which the wort and yeast come together. Because the yeast used is so aggressive and reproduces so quickly, a pipe is attached to each cask to raise the foaming liquid to a trough fitted above. Excess yeast congregates here, with any beer collected dropping back into the cask below. Yorkshire squares are in use at Samuel Smith's brewery in Tadcaster. Developed, as their name suggests, in this part of the country, the squares are fermenting vessels made of slate. Like the Burton unions, they have a second chamber above. However, unlike in Burton, this is because the local yeast is generally slow at doing its job. In order to keep the yeast active, the beer needs constant rousing, effected by pumping the wort into the upper vessel, where excess yeast is then collected as the wort runs back to the square below. Both systems of fermentation heavily influence the flavours, carbonation and body of beers produced in them.

Acting the Goat

Ever noticed the goat on the labels of certain bock beers? Bock is a German term for a strong lager. It is a style that originated in the northern city of Einbeck, and the term 'bock' is thought to have been derived from the last part of the city's name. However, in German, bock also means 'billy goat', and with a beer so strong it kicks like a goat, many brewers feature a goat on the label as a kind of friendly warning.

The 20 Largest American Craft Breweries

	Brewery	US Barrels*
1	Boston Beer Co	1,868,471
2	Sierra Nevada Brewing Co	786,288
3	New Belgium Brewing Co	661,169
4	Spoetzel Brewery	431,145
5	Deschutes Brewery	204,908
6	IBU**	202,838
7	Matt Brewing Co	182,416
8	Bell's Brewery, Inc	153,973
9	Harpoon Brewery	149,490
10	Boulevard Brewing Co	149,008
11	Dogfish Head Craft Brewery	120,460
12	Alaskan Brewing and Bottling Co	117,100
13	Long Trail Brewing Co***	117,000
14	Stone Brewing Co	115,000
15	Abita Brewing Co	109,100
16	Brooklyn Brewery	108,000
17	Lagunitas Brewing Co	106,000
18	Full Sail Brewing Co	100,848
19	Shipyard Brewing Co	98,142
20	Summit Brewing Co	96,799

*Annual output.

**Now part of North American Breweries. Includes Pyramid and Magic Hat beers.

***Includes Otter Creek beers.

Figures given are for 2010. Source: Brewers Association. A craft brewer was partly defined as a company producing fewer than 2 million barrels a year in 2010 (this threshold has since been raised to 6 million barrels a year).

British Breweries With No Brewhouses

There is a growing band of beer companies that do not own breweries. Generally, they use spare capacity at other breweries or have beers brewed under contract for them. Some are wholesaling companies ordering own-badge brews. Below is an indication of where some beers are actually produced, but such details are, of course, subject to change.

Brewery/Wholesaler	Location	Brewery(ies) Used
Blackwater	Stourbridge, West Midlands	Salopian
BMG	Burton-on-Trent, Staffordshire	Tower
Brancaster	Brancaster Staithe, Norfolk	Beeston
Bridgnorth	Bridgnorth, Shropshire	Holden's
Broughs	Netherton, West Midlands	Olde Swan*
City of Cambridge	Chittering, Cambridgeshire	Elgood's
Compass	Oxford	Cotswold*
Gertie Sweet	Eyton, Wrexham	Plassey*
Green Room	St Austell, Cornwall	Keltek*
Hektors	Southwold, Suffolk	Green Jack
Hoskins	Leicester	Tower
Innis & Gunn	Edinburgh	Belhaven
Knops	Edinburgh	Traditional Scottish Ales
Lichfield	Lichfield, Staffordshire	Tower
Lovibonds	Henley-on-Thames, Oxfordshire	Old Luxters*
Mitchell Krause	Workington, Cumbria	Hepworth
Morrissey Fox	Beverley, East Yorkshire	Unknown
Ridgeway	South Stoke, Oxfordshire	Hepworth/ Cotswold*
Steamin' Billy	Oadby, Leicestershire	Tower*
Steel City	Sheffield, South Yorkshire	Little Ale Cart*
Strangford Lough	Killyleagh, Co. Down	Unknown
Suddaby's	Malton, North Yorkshire	Brown Cow
Suthwyk	Southwick, Hampshire	Oakleaf
Untapped	Cardiff	Whittingtons*
Wicked Hathern	East Leake, Leicestershire	Leek

*Brewed themselves using the brewery's equipment.

The Ultimate Christmas Beer?

One of the world's most fascinating beers is Samichlaus. Created by Swiss company Hürlimann in 1979, it is now in the careful hands of Austrian family brewer Eggenberg, which acquired the beer after Hürlimann was taken over and ceased production. Samichlaus means Santa Claus in Swiss German and it is only ever brewed on 6 December, the feast day of St Nicholas. The beer is then cold matured for the best part of a year before being released for sale the following Christmas. At 14% ABV, it certainly encourages you slip into the mellow festive spirit.

Progressive Beer Duty

Progressive Beer Duty (familiarly known as PBD) was introduced in the UK by Chancellor of the Exchequer Gordon Brown in 2002. The system offers a lower rate of duty to small brewers according to their output, and the current output thresholds which apply – along with the formulae needed to calculate the appropriate duty rate – are as follows.

Brewery Output	Duty Rate
5,000 hl or less	50% of standard duty rate
5001–30,000 hl	P – 2,500 (hl) x standard duty rate ÷ P
30,001–60,000 hl	P – 2,500 (hl) – 8.33% of P in excess of 30,000 hl x standard duty rate ÷ P
60,001 hl and more	Standard duty rate

In the above calculations, P = actual production figure in hl.

Barrel Racing in Burton

First staged in May 1933, the sport of rolling beer barrels through the brewing town of Burton-on-Trent was always quite a spectacle, with 12 men competitively pushing casks along the streets. With the decline of the brewing industry, however, it looked like barrel racing had come to an end. The 2003 race appeared to be the last. Happily, in 2011, the International Barrel Rolling Championship was resurrected by Burton's National Brewery Centre, in a wider format, with women's singles and mixed doubles events added to the original men's singles category.

The Fish and the Ring

The emblem of the Orval Trappist monastery brewery in Belgium is a fish with a ring in its mouth. This recalls a legend from the early days of the abbey, way back in the 11th century. It is said that Countess Mathilda of Tuscany, visiting the site, lost the precious wedding ring given to her by her deceased husband, Godfrey the Hunchback, in a spring. Distraught, Mathilda prayed to the Virgin Mary for its return and, when a trout surfaced, ring in its mouth, she was so overwhelmed and delighted that she declared the area to be 'the golden valley' ('orval'). Water from the same spring still supplies the monastery and brewery.

UK Pub Superlatives

Smallest: The Signal Box, Cleethorpes, Lincolnshire
Largest: The Regal, Cambridge (JD Wetherspoon former cinema)
Highest: Tan Hill Inn, North Yorkshire (1,732 feet above sea level)
Northernmost: Baltasound Hotel, Unst, Shetland
Southernmost: Turk's Head, St Agnes, Isles of Scilly
Oldest*: Ye Olde Trip to Jerusalem, Nottingham (1189)/The Old Ferry Boat, St Ives, Cambridgeshire (possibly 10th century)/Ye Olde Fighting Cocks, St Albans, Hertfordshire (possibly 11th century)
Most Common Name*: The Red Lion/The Crown
Longest Pub Name: The Old Thirteenth Cheshire Astley Volunteer Rifleman Corps Inn, Stalybridge, Greater Manchester

*Record in dispute.

Fried Beer, Anyone?

Hats off to American Mark Zable for discovering yet another way to serve beer. His solution to this ever-perplexing problem? Easy: just deep fry it. Zable launched his great invention at a food fair in Texas in 2010. His recipe calls for beer to be trapped inside a casing of salty, pretzel-like dough. The dough is then fried for around 20 seconds, short enough for the alcohol in the beer not to cook off. The beer inside has been reported as being Guinness or Texas's own Shiner Bock, and the ravioli-like parcels of beer are now even available frozen by mail order.

Beer and Mash

Ever noted the similarity in the names of Britain's most popular malting barley and one its most versatile potatoes? Both the Maris Otter barley strain and the Maris Piper potato were first bred in the 1960s in the laboratories of the Plant Breeding Institute at Trumpington, on the outskirts of Cambridge. It was from the name of the street on which the Institute stood – Maris Lane – that the barley and potato were named.

The Trappist Breweries

Only the seven monastic breweries listed below have official sanction from the Vatican to use the term 'Trappist' on their products. To qualify for Trappist accreditation, the beer must be produced within the confines of the abbey; the monks must at least supervise production; and profits can only be used for the upkeep of the abbey buildings and for good causes. Six of the breweries are in Belgium; one (Koningshoeven) is in The Netherlands. Similar beers produced by commercial breweries for other abbeys under licence may only be known as 'Abbey' beers.

Sint Benedictusabdij de Achelse Kluis (Achel)
Abbaye Notre-Dame de Scourmont (Chimay)
Abdij Onze Lieve Vrouw van Koningshoeven (La Trappe)
Abbaye Notre-Dame d'Orval (Orval)
Abbaye Notre-Dame de Saint-Rémy (Rochefort)
Abdij der Trappisten van Westmalle (Westmalle)
Sint-Sixtusabdij van Westvleteren (Westvleteren)

The Watney Cup

In the early 1970s, just when it was foisting its awful Red keg beer (as the despised Red Barrel had now become) on the British public, Watney's also sponsored a major pre-season football tournament. The Watney Cup was a knock-out event for the two highest scoring teams in each of the four English divisions, excluding those that had been promoted or qualified for Europe. Like Watney's Red, it didn't last long. Derby County, Colchester United, Bristol Rovers and Stoke City were the cup's winners.

Specialist Beer and Food Restaurants

There's a growing awareness around the world that beer and food are perfect partners on the fine dining table. Here are some international establishments recognized for their expertise in beer and food pairing.

De Beyerd, Breda, Netherlands
Bierbistro, Toronto, Canada
De Bistronoom, Ostend, Belgium
Brew Wharf, London, UK
't Brouwershuis, Steenhuffel, Belgium
Den Duyver, Bruges, Belgium
Erasmus, Bruges, Belgium
Fountainhead, Chicago, Illinois, USA
De Heeren van Liedekercke, Denderleeuw, Belgium
Higgins Restaurant, Portland, Oregon, USA
't Hommelhof, Watou, Belgium
Hopleaf Bar, Chicago, Illinois, USA
Novare Res Bier Café, Portland, Maine, USA
The Old Brewery, Greenwich, UK
Restaurant Lucullus, Ostend, Belgium
Restobières, Brussels, Belgium
Schildia, Knokke-Heist, Belgium
Spinnekopke, Brussels, Belgium
The White Horse, Parsons Green, London, UK

Interpreting the Language of a Lager Advert

'Fine'	Thin
'Smooth'	Tasteless
'Refreshing'	Higher water content
'Original'	Existed before 2005
'Traditionally made'	We add as much corn syrup as we did in the Seventies
'Satisfying'	Drink enough and you won't care any more
'The Best'	More 'something' (e.g. yellow) than the rest
'Probably the best'	Not quite as yellow as the rest

Extracted from *Good Beer Guide Belgium* by Tim Webb.

Chronology of International Brewery Openings

1040......Weihenstephan, Germany
1050......Weltenburg, Germany
1328......Augustiner, Germany
1383......Löwenbräu, Germany
1397......Spaten, Germany
1634......Paulaner, Germany
1664......Kronenbourg, France
1719......Bavaria, Netherlands
1747......Palm, Belgium
1753......Warsteiner, Germany
1758......Martens, Belgium
1759......Guinness, Ireland
1784......Van Steenberge, Belgium
1786......Molson, Canada
1791......Bosteels, Belgium
1817......Bitburger, Germany
1833......De Koninck, Belgium
1836......Rodenbach, Belgium
          Westmalle, Belgium
1838......Westvleteren, Belgium
1842......Pilsner Urquell,
          Czech Republic
1846......Kulmbacher, Germany
          Peroni, Italy
1847......Carlsberg, Denmark
1848......Jever, Germany
1850......Silly, Belgium
1856......Zywiec, Poland
1857......Kingfisher, India
1862......Chimay, Belgium
          Coopers, Australia
1864......Heineken, Netherlands
1869......Staropramen,
          Czech Republic
1870......Kaltenberg, Germany
1871......Duvel Moortgat, Belgium

1872......Het Anker, Belgium
1876......Estrella Damm, Spain
          Lefèbvre, Belgium
          Sapporo, Japan
1879......Holsten, Germany
1884......La Trappe, Netherlands
1885......Kirin, Japan
1886......Erdinger, Germany
1888......Foster's, Australia
1889......Asahi, Japan
1892......Verhaeghe, Belgium
1895......Budweiser Budvar,
          Czech Republic
          Castle, South Africa
1898......Haacht, Belgium
1899......Rochefort, Belgium
1900......Cantillon, Belgium
1906......Huyghe, Belgium
1920......Dupont, Belgium
1922......Duyck, France
1928......Farsons, Malta
1931......Orval, Belgium
1935......Affligem, Belgium
1946......St Bernardus, Belgium
1966......Hoegaarden, Belgium
1977......Boon, Belgium
1979......Abbaye des Rocs, Belgium
1980......De Dolle, Belgium
1982......Achouffe, Belgium
1990......Baltika, Russia
1996......Baladin, Italy
          Birrificio Italiano, Italy
          Proef, Belgium
1998......Achel, Netherlands
2000......Little Creatures, Australia
2006......Ducato, Italy

Note: See Who Owns Whom, pages 40–41, for details of current ownership.

CAMRA's Prices' Survey Results

Year	Real Ale	Lager	Dearest Region	Cheapest Region
1994	147	163	165	129
1995	155	173	169	134
1996	160	179	174	140
1997	164	179	179	143
1998	171	187	192	147
1999	176	193	193	153
2000	182	201	195	155
2001	186	206	206	165
2002	192	211	212	169
2003	198	217	215	175
2004	206	225	224	187
2005	215	236	236	184
2006	224	245	242	197
2007	234	257	257	204
2008	245	265	264	215
2009	258	279	279	226
2010	268	293	292	224
2011	284	302	315	247

Figures are an average of UK prices for real ale and lager, plus average real ale prices in the dearest and cheapest UK regions (usually London and North-West England, respectively). Prices are given in pence.

Gone for a Burton

During World War II, RAF aircrew adopted a euphemism to disguise their sadness when one of their colleagues failed to return from a mission. 'He's gone for a Burton,' they'd say, implying he'd just nipped out for a pint and referring – it is believed – to a now almost-forgotten style of beer produced originally in Burton-on-Trent. The beer should not be confused with Burton's other great exports, namely pale ale and India pale ale. This was a darker, sweeter brew, perhaps best exemplified today by Young's Winter Warmer, or the stronger bottled beer Marston's Owd Rodger. There are other explanations suggested for the origin of this now commonly-used phrase, but naturally we prefer the beer one.

The UK's Most Successful Brewers and Beers

Based on results collated from CAMRA's annual Champion Beer of Britain and Champion Winter Beer of Britain competitions, here are the UK's most successful brewers. The figures are correct up to and including the 2011 Champion Beer and Champion Winter Beer contests.

Most Supreme Champion Titles

Brewery	Wins	Last Win
Fuller's	5	1989*
Taylor	4	1999
Crouch Vale	2	2006
Nethergate	2	2003**
Robinson's	2	2005**
Thwaites	2	1980*
Woodforde's	2	1996

*Includes one shared title.

**Champion Winter Beer of Britain titles.

Most Category Wins

Brewery	Wins	Last Win
Fuller's	13	2007
Taylor	12	2010
Batemans	10	2005
Woodforde's	8	2005
Hop Back	6	2011
Gale's	5	2006
Oakham	5	2002
RCH	5	2010
Robinson's	5	2010
Theakston's	5	2000
Harveys	4	2006
Nethergate	4	2009
Adnams	3	2003
Ansells	3	1987
Cairngorm	3	2006
Cheriton	3	2003
Coach House	3	1994
Mighty Oak	3	2011

O'Hanlon's	3	2007
Ridley's	3	1995
Thwaites	3	1986
Triple fff	3	2008
Wye Valley	3	2008
Young's	3	1999

Most Successful Beers*

Beer	Wins	Last Win
Taylor Landlord	9	2010
Fuller's ESB	7	1991
Batemans XXXB	5	1997
Theakston's Old Peculier	5	2000
Hop Back Summer Lightning	4	2001
Cairngorm Trade Winds	3	2006
Gale's Festival Mild	3	2006
Nethergate Old Growler	3	2003**
Woodforde's Headcracker	3	2003
Woodforde's Wherry	3	2005
Worthington's White Shield	3	2006

*Based on category wins.

**Includes one shared title.

Beer Escapology

The world's most famous escapologist, Harry Houdini, pulled off countless dramatic escapes from sealed boxes and milk churns filled with water, but beer very nearly proved to be his downfall. While touring Britain in 1911, Houdini accepted a challenge from Tetley's Brewery in Leeds to be immersed in a churn filled with beer instead of water. However, the great man was overcome by carbon dioxide and it required a sharp-witted assistant to extract him from the ale. It wasn't Houdini's last encounter with beer, however. Despite obvious reluctance to attempt such a challenge again, he nevertheless picked up the gauntlet thrown down by Standard Brewing of Scranton, Pennsylvania (where a Houdini museum is now open), and allowed himself to be trapped in a cask of its Tru-Age ale. This time, thankfully, beer was not his master and he extricated himself without trouble from a potential beery grave.

Societies Dedicated to Brewing and Pub History

Brewery History Society
An apolitical body dedicated to recording Britain's brewing heritage.
www.breweryhistory.com

Inn Sign Society
Organization founded in 1990 to record information about inn signs
and pub names. www.innsignsociety.com

Society for the Preservation of Beers from the Wood
Founded in 1963; now a general cask ale appreciation society.
www.spbw.com

Pub History Society
Body established in 2001 to bring together keen pub historians and
researchers. www.pubhistory.freeserve.co.uk

Systems of Running a Pub

Traditionally, pubs in Britain have been operated in two ways. The first
is the free house, in which the pub is owned by the licensee who is free
to sell whichever beers he or she chooses. However, some 'free houses'
also have a financial arrangement with a brewery, which may limit the
choice of beers on sale. The second is the tied house, in which a pub is
owned by a brewery and is tied to selling only that brewery's products
(plus any guest beers supplied by the brewery). Tied houses break down
into managed and tenanted pubs. A managed pub is run for the brewery
by a paid employee of the brewery. A tenanted pub is run by a licensee
who has contracted to run the business for a short period of time
(generally three, or perhaps five, years). In recent decades, tenanted
pubs have become rare, as breweries have moved to a system of longer
leases (often lasting around 20 years) with usually less favourable terms
than offered for the traditional tenancy. The picture is obscured further
by the arrival in the last 20 years of major pub-owning companies that
have acquired pubs that were once owned and run by breweries. These
companies also operate pubs on a managed or leased basis, with
controls on beer supply (or at least some part of it) commonly in force.

A Pint of Old

It seems that a pint of old is subject to the most ridiculous names. Here are some of the more bizarre names over the years from British brewers.

Beer	Brewery
Old Accidental	Brunswick
Old Bat	B&T
Old Big 'Ead	Wild Walker
Old Bloomer	Concrete Cow
Old Buffer	Garton
Old Cantankerous	Tring
Old Clog	Mitchell's
Old Cock Up	Nix Wincott
Old Cock's Throat Charmer	Hop House
Old Codger	Rebellion
Old Croak	Frog & Parrot
Old Dark Attic	Concertina
Old Dray	Worldham
Old E'fer	Brown Cow
Old Engine Oil	Harviestoun
Old Expensive	Burton Bridge
Old Fart	Robinwood
Old Fecker	Grindleton
Old Forgetful	Green Dragon
Old Fossil	Stony Rock
Old Gaffer	DarkTribe
Old Gavel Bender	Judges
Old Goat	Cropton
Old Growler	Nethergate
Old Groyne	Willy's
Old Grumblebelly	Cheriton
Old Herbaceous	Rockingham
Old Horny	Blythe
Old Horse Whip	Mildmay
Old Jock Strap	Greenwood
Old Knobbley	Arbor
Old Knuckle Shuffler	Boat

Beer	Brewery
Old Lag	Marble
Old Lech	Halfpenny
Old Leg Over	Daleside
Old Lubrication	Daleside
Old Ma Weasel	Ales of Kent
Old Moggie	Teignworthy
Old Mortality	Strathaven
Old Mottled Cock	Leadmill
Old Needle's Eye	Unicorn Inn
Old Pecker	Ballard's
Old Peculier	Theakston
Old Pedantic	Sutton
Old Pondwater	Yates
Old Recumbent	Six Bells
Old Red Eye	Brown Cow
Old Remedial	Moulin
Old Rodent	Summerskills
Old Rot	Quay
Old Scatness	Valhalla
Old Sea Dog	Bushy's
Old Slapper	Bank Top
Old Slug Porter	RCH
Old Soporific	West Coast
Old Speckled Hen	Greene King
Old Speckled Parrot	Wheal Ale
Old Stoatwobbler	Spectrum
Old Stone Trough	Ryburn
Old Tackle	Chalk Hill
Old Thumper	Ringwood
Old Thunderbox	Green Jack
Old Tosser	Smiles/Oyster
Old Trout	Kemptown
Olde Home Wrecker	Milestone

Top Fermentation and Bottom Fermentation

The beer world broadly splits into two sectors: beers that are top fermented and beers that are bottom fermented. These terms refer to the activity of the yeast. Some strains of yeast generally sit on top of the wort as it ferments, while others sink to the bottom. Top fermentation is used for ale production, while bottom fermentation is associated mostly with lagers. Here are the beer styles on either side of the divide.

Top-Fermented Styles	Bottom-Fermented Styles
Ales	Lagers
Stouts	Pilsners
Porters	Viennas
Weissbiers	Rauchbiers
Witbiers	Bocks
Berliner Weisse	Dortmunder
Lambics	Märzen

The European Beer Consumers Union

The European Beer Consumers Union (EBCU) was founded in 1990. It is a federation of national beer consumer groups whose objectives are the promotion of Europe's beer culture and traditional beer styles, as well as championing diversity and consumer choice, enhancing the image of beer and representing consumers' interests. These are current members.

Austria: BierIG	www.bierig.org
Belgium: *Zythos*	www.zythos.be
Czech Republic: *Sdruzeni Pratel Pivne*	www.pratelepiva.cz
Denmark: *Danske Ølentusiaster*	www.ale.dk
Finland: *Olutliitto*	www.olutliitto.fi
Italy: *Unionbirrai*	www.unionbirrai.com
The Netherlands: PINT	www.pint.nl
Norway: NORØL	www.nor-ale.org
Poland: *Bractwo Piwne*	www.bractwopiwne.pl
Sweden: *Svenska Ölfrämjandet*	www.svenskaolframjandet.se
Switzerland: *Association des Buveurs d'Orges*	www.abo-ch.org
UK: CAMRA	www.camra.org.uk

Beer Heroes: John Young (1921–2006)

In the dark days of the early 1970s, when British breweries were turning their backs on traditional cask-conditioned ale in favour of high-profit, low-maintenance keg beers, one brewery stood defiant. Young's of Wandsworth, London, never allowed its horse-drawn drays to carry dead, pasteurized ale and central to this admirable policy was long-serving brewery chairman John Young. Even after cask beer had made a comeback, Young continued to fight the good fight. He was often seen posing for publicity photographs in a Young's pub or at a company AGM, extolling the virtues of great British beer dressed as a boxer or perhaps even Father Christmas. The world of beer lost a true champion when John Young died. It was significant that his life slipped away the week the final brew was mashed in at Young's, following a board decision to close the site and transfer brewing to Bedford. With John Young's passing, British brewing undoubtedly became a greyer place.

Some Rescued Beers

When breweries are taken over and closed, some of the beers are often continued under the new ownership (at least for a while). Some beers also survive breweries that are closed in other circumstances, with rival companies cherry picking brands worth preserving. Here are examples.

Beer	Original Brewery	Current Brewery
The Bishop's Tipple	Gibbs Mew	Wadworth
Double Maxim	Vaux	Double Maxim
Lancaster Bomber	Mitchell's	Thwaites
Pompey Royal	Brickwood's	Oakleaf
Royal Oak	Eldridge Pope	O'Hanlon's
Waggle Dance	Vaux	Wells & Young's

Barmy Bread

A speciality in northern England, barm cakes are bread rolls traditionally made with 'barm' – fresh yeast skimmed from fermenting beer. Yeast is also the source of the word 'barmy', meaning 'froth headed' or crazy.

UK Breweries Still Employing Coopers

A cooper is a maker and repairer of wooden casks, a position that has been lost at nearly all breweries since the arrival of metal containers. In addition to the four breweries mentioned below, other breweries also occasionally offer 'beer from the wood' but do not employ a cooper.

Marston's*   Samuel Smith   T&R Theakston   Wadworth

*Not for casks for delivery but for the upkeep of the casks used in the Burton Union fermentation system.

The Bottled Beer Revival

In 1987, the Campaign for Real Ale's *Good Beer Guide* made one of its more pessimistic and, thankfully, less successful predictions. In a feature on bottled beers it claimed that 'by the end of the century Britain's remaining breweries will produce between them no more than a dozen bottled beers'.

But look around you as you visit your local off-licence or supermarket. Far from having only a dozen beers under glass as we head towards the Millennium, we have never been so blessed with bottles. Most contain foreign lagers or brewery processed ales but an increasing number now offer beer which is naturally conditioned in the bottle – in other words, real ale. And that's where this new guide comes in.

For a number of years the CAMRA *Good Beer Guide* has listed which bottle-conditioned beers are brewed by Britain's breweries, but, apart from a stark mention of the original gravities and alcohol by volume figures, that's all the *Good Beer Guide* – with its focus, justifiably, on cask real ale and the pubs which sell it – has had room to provide. The CAMRA *Good Bottled Beer Guide* is intended as a companion book to the *Good Beer Guide*, filling the void in coverage of the bottled real ale scene. Five or six years ago, the fact that this book didn't exist was a matter of little concern. There were, after all, a mere handful of bottle-conditioned beers available in the UK. Now all that has changed and the publication of such a book is more than overdue.

From the introduction to the first-ever CAMRA *Good Bottled Beer Guide*, published 1998. The book discovered around 180 bottle-conditioned beers; the seventh edition, published in 2009, featured more than 1,300.

Painting is Thirsty Work

'When we returned in the fall, the house was as empty as a beer closet in premises where painters have been at work.'

The McWilliamses and the Burglar Alarm, Mark Twain

Fruits Commonly Used in Fruit Lambics

Belgium's lambic beers are spontaneously fermented by wild yeasts in the environment and have a tart, earthy flavour. Some of these beers are also laced with fruit, which introduces new fermentable sugars and encourages a further fermentation. The styles created are shown below.

Fruit	Name of Style
Cherries	Kriek
Raspberries	Frambozen/Framboise
Blackcurrants	Cassis
Peaches	Pêche

International Beer Challenge

The International Beer Challenge is a major competition for packaged beer (bottle and can), staged in London each year and closely allied to the trade magazine *Off Licence News*. Gold, silver and bronze awards are made in various classes but a supreme champion beer is always selected, too. Below is a list of the supreme champions in recent years.

2003	Weihenstephaner Hefeweissbier
2004	Innis & Gunn Oak Aged Beer
2005	Rogue Mocha Porter"
2006	O'Hanlon's Thomas Hardy's Ale
2007	Deschutes The Abyss
2008	St Austell Admiral's Ale
2009	Weihenstephaner Hefeweissbier
2010	Boston Beer Samuel Adams Utopias 2009
2011	Kernel Export Stout

Twenty-Five Years of Major UK Brewery Closures

1987 .... Dryborough, Edinburgh (Watney)
Rayments, Furneaux Pelham (Greene King)

1988 .... Paines, St Neots (Tolly Cobbold)
Theakston's, Carlisle (Matthew Brown)
Chester's, Salford (Whitbread)
Wem, Shropshire (Greenalls)
Theakston's, Workington (Scottish & Newcastle)
Wethered, Marlow (Whitbread)

1989 .... Davenports, Birmingham (Greenalls)
Truman, London (Grand Metropolitan)

1990 .... Crown, Pontyclun (Guinness)
Fremlins, Faversham (Whitbread)
Higsons, Liverpool
(Whitbread – now re-opened as Cains)

1991 .... Hansons, Dudley (Wolverhampton & Dudley)
Hartleys, Ulverston (Robinson's)
Greenalls, Warrington (ceased brewing)
Matthew Brown, Blackburn (Scottish & Newcastle)
Preston Brook, Runcorn (Bass)
Shipstone's, Nottingham (Greenalls)
Springfield, Wolverhampton (Bass)
Romford (Allied Breweries)

1993 .... Exchange, Sheffield (Whitbread)

1994 .... Heriot, Edinburgh (Bass)
Hope, Sheffield (Bass)

1996 .... Plympton, Plymouth (Carlsberg-Tetley)
Tetley Walker, Warrington (Carlsberg-Tetley)
Webster's, Halifax (Scottish & Newcastle)
Home, Nottingham (Scottish & Newcastle)

1997 .... Gibbs Mew, Salisbury (ceased brewing)

1998 .... Crown Buckley, Llanelli (Brains)
Cheltenham (Whitbread)
Morrells, Oxford (ceased brewing)
Ruddles, Oakham (Morland)

1999 .... Alloa (Carlsberg-Tetley)
Vaux, Sunderland (ceased brewing)
Wards, Sheffield (Vaux)

Mitchell's, Lancaster (ceased brewing)
Wrexham Lager (Carlsberg-Tetley)
Courage, Bristol (Scottish & Newcastle)
Cannon, Sheffield (Bass)
Brains, Cardiff (company moved after taking over Welsh
Brewers brewery from Bass)
Maclay's, Alloa (ceased brewing)

2000 .... Morland, Abingdon (Greene King)
King & Barnes, Horsham (Hall & Woodhouse)
Ushers, Trowbridge (ceased brewing)

2001 .... Mansfield (Wolverhampton & Dudley)

2002 .... Cape Hill, Birmingham (Coors)
Castle Eden (brewing moved to Camerons in Hartlepool)
Brakspear, Henley-on-Thames (ceased brewing)

2003 .... Thomas Hardy, Dorchester (brewing moved to
Burtonwood)
Tolly Cobbold, Ipswich (brands sold to Ridley's)

2004 .... Fountain, Edinburgh (Scottish & Newcastle)

2005 .... Boddingtons, Manchester (InBev)
Park Royal, London (Guinness)
Redruth, Cornwall (ceased brewing)
Tyne, Newcastle-upon-Tyne (Scottish & Newcastle)

2006 .... Gale's, Horndean (Fuller's)
Hardy's & Hanson's, Nottingham (Greene King)
Ridley's, Hartford End (Greene King)
Young's, Wandsworth (brewing merged with Charles Wells)

2010 .... Dunston (Heineken UK)
Highgate, Walsall (ceased brewing)
Reading (Heineken UK)

2011 .... Tetley, Leeds (Carlsberg UK)

The list covers major breweries only. Names in brackets indicate the company that closed
the brewery.

Chairmen of the British Guild of Beer Writers

1988–91	Michael Jackson	**2000–3**	Roger Protz
1991–8	Barrie Pepper	**2003–6**	Andrew Pring
1998–2000	Susan Nowak	**2006–**	Tim Hampson

ABW and ABV

In some parts of the world (including the USA), alcohol content for beer has traditionally been declared as an ABW – Alcohol by Weight – figure, showing the number of grammes of alcohol per 100 grammes of the liquid (alcohol is lighter than water). However, brewers are increasingly using the international system of ABV – Alcohol by Volume – which shows the percentage of alcohol in the liquid. To convert from ABW to ABV, just multiply by 1.25 (consequently a beer of 4% ABW = 5% ABV). To convert the other way, from ABV to ABW, simply multiply by 0.8.

Famous Hop Growing Regions

Region	Strains (examples)	Harvest
Bohemia, Czech Republic	Saaz	August
Hallertau, Bavaria, Germany	Hersbrucker/Magnum	August
Herefordshire, UK	Fuggle/Golding/Target	September
Kent, UK	Challenger/Golding/Target	September
New Zealand	Green Bullet/Sticklebract	February–March
Slovenia	Bobek/Celeia/Savinjski Golding	August–September
Tasmania, Australia	Pride of Ringwood	March–April
Worcestershire, UK	Fuggle/Golding/Target	September
Yakima, Washington, USA	Cascade/Cluster/Willamette	August–September

Drink Celtic

Forging a bibulous link with the past every November is St Austell brewery's Celtic Beer Festival. Since 1999, the Victorian cellars and vaults beneath the Cornwall brewhouse have played host to a one-day extravaganza of beers brewed in Celtic regions. More than 100 beers – a mixture of regular and special brews – are now offered from breweries in Scotland, Wales, Ireland, Isle of Man, Cornwall and Brittany. Live music also features and all proceeds go to boost the St Austell Charitable Trust.

Some Daft Beer Names Past and Present

Name	Brewery	Country
Arrogant Bastard Ale	Stone	US
Baz's Bonce Blower	Parish	UK
Blithering Idiot	Weybacher	US
Buttface Amber Ale	Big Horn	US
Cross Buttock	Jennings	UK
Delirium Tremens	Huyghe	Belgium
Dog's Bollocks	Wychwood	UK
Dog's in't Barrel	Old Spot	UK
Elbow Grease	Summer Wine	UK
Fancy Lawnmower	St Arnold	US
Fat Bastard	River City/Silver City	US
Fat Tire	New Belgium	US
Fox's Nob	Highgate	UK
Funky Monkey	Milk Street	UK
Fursty Ferret	Hall & Woodhouse	UK
Golden Showers	Dartmouth/Son of Sid	UK
Granny Wouldn't Like It	Wolf	UK
Hairy Helmet	Leatherbritches	UK
Ich Bin ein Berliner Weisse	Nodding Head Brewing	US
Jean Cloudy Van Damme	Tunnel	UK
Kilt Sniffer	Big Dog's Brewing	US
Kripple Dick	Keltek	UK
Moose Drool	Big Sky	US
Mother-in-Law's Tongue Tied	Bartrams	UK
No-Eye Deer	Goose Eye	UK
Piddle in the Wind	Wyre Piddle	UK
Pigs Ass Porter	Harvest Moon	US
Pressed Rat & Warthog	Triple fff	UK
Rip Snorter	Hog's Back	UK
Santa's Butt	Ridgeway	UK
Side Pocket for a Toad	Tring	UK
Son of a Bitch	Bullmastiff	UK
Spank Dog	Ninkasi Brewing	US
Spicy Fish Wife	Slip Point	US
Tabatha the Knackered	Anglo Dutch	UK
Tactical Nuclear Penguin	BrewDog	UK

Beers Granted European Union PGI Status

Protected Geographical Indication (PGI) status is open to products which must be produced or processed or prepared within a defined geographical area and have a reputation, features or certain qualities attributable to that area. Other foods with this accreditation include Welsh lamb; Whitstable oysters; Dorset Blue and Camembert cheeses; Parma ham; Jersey Royal potatoes; and pork pies from Melton Mowbray.

Czech Beers:
Černá Hora
Březnický Ležák
Brněnské Pivo; Starobrněnské Pivo
Znojemské Pivo
České Pivo
Chodské Pivo
Budějovické Pivo
Budějovický Měšťanský Var
Českobudějovické Pivo

German Beers:
Bayerisches Bier
Bremer Bier
Dortmunder Bier
Hofer Bier
Kölsch
Kulmbacher Bier
Mainfranken Bier
Münchener Bier
Reuther Bier
Wernesgrüner Bier

UK Beers:
Kentish Ale and Kentish Strong Ale*
Rutland Bitter**

*Submitted by Shepherd Neame.

**Submitted by Ruddles Brewery. Ruddles beers are now brewed at Greene King in Bury St Edmunds and can no longer be termed Rutland Bitter.

Note: Newcastle Brown Ale held PGI status until 2007, when its owner, Scottish Courage, asked for a repeal in order to brew the beer outside Newcastle-upon-Tyne.

The US Beer Market

	No. of Breweries	Million US Barrels	Market Share
US Non-Craft Brewers	43	166.54	81.81%
Imports	-	27.14	13.33%
Craft Brewers*	1716	9.95	4.86%

*Includes brewpubs. 2010 figures. Source: Brewers Association.

Some Beer Cocktails

Bee Sting (stout and orange juice)
Black and Tan (stout and bitter/mild)
Black Velvet (stout and champagne)
Boilermaker (beer and a shot of whisky)
Broadway (beer and cola)
Cooper (stout and porter)
Depth Charge (beer with a submerged glass of whisky)
Dog's Nose (bitter and a shot of gin)
Flip (beer, gin, sugar and eggs)
Liverpool Kiss (stout and cassis)
Mother-in-Law (old and bitter or stout and bitter)
Red Eye (beer and a shot of tomato juice)
Shandy (bitter and lemonade)
Skip and Go Naked (beer, lemon juice, gin and grenadine)
Snakebite (beer and cider)

Full Circle for the Most Travelled Beer

The history of Worthington's White Shield is one of relocation, relocation, relocation. Having been created by Worthington in Burton-on-Trent in the 1820s, this classic bottle-conditioned beer became part of the Bass empire in 1927 and during the late 20th century was sent on its travels. As volumes declined, the beer was shipped out of Burton and given a new home at the Hope Brewery in Sheffield. When this closed in 1994, Bass moved it to its Cape Hill brewery in Birmingham. With sales still in decline, the beer was officially discontinued in 1997. Public protest led to Bass having a change of heart and passing on the brewing, sales and marketing of the brand to King & Barnes in Horsham, West Sussex. In 2000, King & Barnes was taken over and closed by Hall & Woodhouse, leaving the beer homeless again. At last recognizing its potential (under King & Barnes, White Shield had been judged CAMRA's champion bottle-conditioned beer), Bass took it home to Burton, installing the beer at the exhibition brewery within the Bass Museum, which was renamed the White Shield Brewery. Interest continued to grow, sales increased and, in 2010, Molson Coors (the latest owner of various former Bass brands) took the beer back into its main brewhouse.

Principles of Beer and Food Pairing

1   Match the weight of the beer against the weight of the food. Don't overpower the food with a beer that is too robust, nor overpower the beer with food that is too rich or strong tasting. Thinking of pale beer as white wine and darker beers as red wine may help in this respect.

2   Look for complements and contrasts. Match flavours in the beer to similar flavours in the food (e.g. roasted or fruit notes), or engineer a contrast such as a chef does with sauces (e.g. a fruit beer with venison, a lemon-accented beer with fish).

3   Use beers to cleanse the palate where possible. A sharp hoppiness or acidity can slice through fat and grease, and lively carbonation can scrub the tongue clean after creamy dishes.

4   Don't bring out the big beers too early; try to build up in terms of character and strength.

5   Be sensible with quantities, especially as beer is carbonated. No one wants to lose their appetite through being bloated.

The Diplomatic Beer Exchange

In July 2010, at the G8/G20 Summit held in Canada, US President Barack Obama and UK Prime Minister David Cameron settled a bet. Only a month earlier, the two leaders had enjoyed friendly rivalry as England took on the USA during the soccer World Cup in South Africa, agreeing a small wager on the outcome. With the game ending in a draw, neither was able to claim bragging rights, or the prize case of beer, but they agreed to swap drinks anyway, choosing to offer beers brewed close to their political power bases. Obama presented Cameron with a case of Goose Island 312 from Chicago, Illinois, the state for which he had been previously senator. In return, Cameron handed over a case of Wychwood Hobgoblin, brewed in his parliamentary constituency of Witney, in Oxfordshire. The friendly exchange of beverages helped break the ice as the two men settled down to their first major face-to-face discussions.

The Wayfarer's Dole

There is such a thing as free beer. Pay a visit to the Hospital of St Cross in Winchester, England, and, on request, you'll be presented with a cup of ale and a small cube of bread. The Wayfarer's Dole, as this generosity is known, dates back centuries to when the Hospital – a term used in its ancient sense to mean a place of hospitality – stood on an important pilgrims' route. Britain's oldest charitable institution, the Hospital dates back to the 12th century and its almshouse is still home to a community of elderly 'brothers' who appreciate its good works. But anyone can benefit from the Hospital's largesse. Just ask at the porter's lodge and a small serving of ale (currently Fuller's London Pride) is yours. Of course, you can then return the favour by buying something in the souvenir shop that helps support the Hospital's upkeep and works.

British Brewery Name Changes

The following breweries have all changed their names at some point.

Old Name	New Name	Old Name	New Name
Alehouse	Verulam	Lidstone's	Wensleydale
Ales of Kent	Four Alls	Maldon	Farmer's Ales
Ann Street	Jersey	McLaughlin	Camden Town
Banks & Taylor	B&T	Oak	Phoenix
Barron's	Exe Valley	Organic	Chough
Big End	Daleside	Paradise	North Wales
Bramcote	Castle Rock	Pennine	Rossendale
Brothers	Freedom	Princetown	Dartmoor
Bunces	Stonehenge	Quay	Dorset
Captain Grumpy's	Wissey Valley	Royal Clarence	RCH
Doghouse	All Saints	Somerset Electric	Taunton
Eastwood & Sanders	Elland	Spinning Dog	Hereford
Flagship	Nelson	Stationhouse	Frodsham
Four Rivers	Hadrian & Border	Sutton	South Hams
Fowler's	Prestonpans	Taunton Vale	Taunton
Gargoyles	Isca	Topsham & Exeter	Exeter
Glenny	Wychwood	Wem	Shropshire
Highwood	Tom Wood	Worfield	Shires

American Beer/Craft Beer Weeks

To entrench the revival of great brewing in the USA and Canada, a number of cities and states now host week-long (sometimes longer) celebrations of fine beer. Events include brewery tours, beer festivals, beer and food pairings, meet the brewer evenings and more. The exact dates may vary but here is a basic calendar to help you plan your visit!

Month	City/State
February	Cincinnati, Ohio
	Sacramento, California
	San Francisco, California
March	Charlotte, North Carolina
April	Albuquerque, New Mexico
	Colorado
	Madison, Wisconsin
	Milwaukee, Wisconsin
May	American Craft Beer Week (national)
	Boston, Massachusetts
	Chicago, Illinois
	Eugene, Oregon
	Frederick, Maryland
	Minnesota
	Seattle, Washington
	Vancouver, British Columbia
June	Alabama
	Ontario
	Philadelphia, Pennsylvania
July	Ohio
August	St Louis, Missouri
	Washington, DC
September	Louisville, Kentucky
	New York
	Toronto, Ontario
October	Baltimore, Maryland
	Cleveland, Ohio
	Los Angeles, California
November	San Diego, California
	Syracuse, New York

Some Cask Terminology

Bilge	The central and widest point of the cask
Bunghole	The hole in the head of a cask through which it is filled
Bush	Brass insert in a wooden cask to hold the keystone or shive
Keystone	Wooden or nylon stopper for the tap hole, with a centre that can be knocked through to fit a tap
Shive	Wooden or nylon stopper to fit the bunghole
Spile	Wooden peg that allows carbon dioxide to be vented off; a hard spile is much less porous than a soft spile
Tut	Central part of the shive that can be knocked through to fit a spile

The Independent Family Brewers of Britain

The Independent Family Brewers of Britain (IFBB) is an association of surviving family brewers, founded in 1993 to promote and protect the historic and community values of the UK's independent breweries, the pubs they operate and the beers they produce. Member companies are:

Arkell's Brewery Ltd
George Bateman & Son Ltd
WH Brakspear & Sons Ltd*
Black Sheep Brewery plc
Daniel Batham & Son Ltd
SA Brain & Co Ltd
Donnington Brewery
Elgood & Sons Ltd
Everards Brewery Ltd
Felinfoel Brewery Co Ltd
Fuller, Smith & Turner plc
Hall & Woodhouse Ltd
Harvey & Son (Lewes) Ltd
Holden's Brewery Ltd
Joseph Holt Ltd

Hook Norton Brewery Co Ltd
Hydes Brewery Ltd
JW Lees & Co (Brewers) Ltd
McMullen & Sons Ltd
JC & RH Palmer Ltd
Frederic Robinson Ltd
St Austell Brewery Co Ltd
Shepherd Neame Ltd
Timothy Taylor & Co Ltd
T&R Theakston Ltd
Daniel Thwaites plc
Wadworth & Co Ltd
Charles Wells Ltd**
Young & Co's Brewery plc**

*Now a pub company. **Although Wells and Young's amalgamated their brewing interests in 2006, they retain individual membership.

CAMRA's Pub Design Awards

In conjunction with English Heritage, CAMRA recognizes good pub architecture through its Pub Design Awards, which are presented in five categories. Here are the winners since the awards were inaugurated.

Year	Best New Pub	Best Refurbishment
1983	—	Bricklayers Arms, London W1/Britannia Inn, Oswaldtwistle
1984	—	Argyll Arms, London W1/Lincoln Arms, Weybridge/Boar's Head, Leigh/Prince Arthur, Walton/Albion, Leeds/Waggon & Horses, Brierfield
1985	Harrier, Peterborough	Olde Spa Inne, Derby
1986	Barn Owl, Northampton	Minerva, Hull/Chandos, London WC2
1987	—	—
1988	No awards	
1989	—	Sun Inn, Barnes/Bow Bar, Edinburgh
1990	—	White Hart, Littleton-on-Severn
1991	Smiles Brewery Tap, Bristol	—
1992	Blind Jack's, Knaresborough	Anchor, Oxford
1993	—	IW Frazier's Cumberland Bar, Edinburgh
1994	—	Cain's Brewery Tap, Liverpool
1995	—	Seahorse, Bristol
1996	—	—
1997	—	Bread & Roses, London SW4
1998	Wharf, Walsall	Stalybridge Station Buffet
1999	—	Dispensary, Liverpool
2000	—	—
2001	—	Burton Bridge Brewery Tap, Burton-on-Trent
2002	Manor Barn Farm, Southfleet	Test Match, West Bridgford
2003	—	Wortley Almshouses, Peterborough
2004	No awards	
2005	Zerodegrees, Bristol	Racecourse, Salford
2006	—	Prince of Wales, Herne Bay
2007	Black Horse Inn, Walcote	Weaver Hotel, Runcorn
2008	Zerodegrees, Reading	Princess Louise, London/Castle Inn, Bradford on Avon
2009	—	Sutton Hall, Macclesfield
2010	—	Bell Inn, Rode

*Sponsored by English Heritage and rewards conservation of a pub's best architectural features and preservation of its fabric.

**Award named after a former CAMRA chairman and presented for the best street-corner local, if worthy.

Note: Awards are not made in every category every year.

Best Conversion to Pub	Conservation Award*	Joe Goodwin Award**
–	–	–
–	–	–
–	–	Howcroft, Bolton
–	–	Crown Posada, Newcastle-upon-Tyne/Scotch Piper, Lydiate
–	–	Golden Cross, Cardiff
–	–	Junction, Southampton
–	–	Queen's Head, Stockport
–	Mill of the Black Monks, Monks Bretton	–
–	–	–
Truscott, London EC2	Fox & Anchor, London EC1	–
–	Bridge Inn, Rochdale	Bridge Inn, Rochdale
Rothwells, Manchester/Courtyard, Leeds	Counting House, Pontefract	–
Commercial Rooms, Bristol	Commercial Rooms, Bristol	Vine, Brierly Hill
Frazer's Bar, Edinburgh	–	–
–	Olde Trip to Jerusalem, Nottingham	–
Billiard Hall, West Bromwich/Half Moon, London E1	–	Dispensary, Liverpool
Sedge Lynn, Manchester	Phoenix, York	Monkey, Crewe
Porterhouse, London	Bull & Butcher, Turville	Merchants Arms, Bristol
Gatekeeper, Cardiff	Bath Hotel, Sheffield	Holt's Railway, Didsbury
Smiths of Bourne, Lincolnshire	Bell Inn, Nottingham	–
Yorkshire Terrier, York	Prestoungrange Gothenberg, Prestonpans	Yarborough Hunt, Brigg
Works, Sowerby Bridge	Three Pigeons, Halifax	Prince of Wales, Herne Bay/Three Pigeons, Halifax
Tobie Norris, Stamford	Weaver Hotel, Runcorn	–
–	–	–
Brewery Tap, Chester	Brewery Tap, Chester	–
Sheffield Tap, Sheffield	Sportsman, Huddersfield	Queen's Head, Burnham on Crouch

Abbey Beer Brands

Belgian beers that are produced commercially for an abbey under licence, or for sale under abbey names, are known as 'Abbey' beers. The breweries at which they are produced are revealed in the following list.

Beer	Brewery
Affligem	Affligem (Heineken)
Aulne	Val de Sambre
Bonne Esperance	Lefèbvre
Bornem	Van Steenberge
Cambron	Silly
Dendermonde	De Block
Ename	Roman
Floreffe	Lefèbvre
Grimbergen	Alken-Maes (Heineken)
Keizersberg	Van Steenberge
Leffe	Stella Artois (A-B InBev)
Maredsous	Duvel Moortgat
Postel	Affligem (Heineken)
St Feuillien	St Feuillien
St Idesbald	Huyghe
St Martin	Brunehaut
Steenbrugge	Palm
Tongerlo	Haacht
Val-Dieu	Val-Dieu

Beer Ingredients in Other Languages

Ingredient	French	Dutch	German	Italian	Portuguese	Spanish
Water	Eau	Water	Wasser	Acqua	Água	Agua
Barley	Orge	Gerst	Gerste	Orzo	Cevada	Cerbada
Malt	Malt	Mout	Malz	Malto	Malte	Malte
Hop	Houblon	Hop	Hopfen	Luppolo	Lúpulo	Lúpulo
Yeast	Levure	Gist	Hefe	Lievito	Levedura	Levadura
Oats	Avoine	Haver	Hafen	Avena	Aveia	Avena
Rye	Seigle	Rogge	Roggen	Segale	Centeio	Centeno
Wheat	Blé/Froment	Tarwe	Weizen	Frumento	Trigo	Trigo

Brewery on Its Bike

New Belgium brewery in Fort Collins, Colorado, was set up after its founder Jeff Lebesch enjoyed a cycling tour of Belgium. Fittingly, the company is still big on bikes. As well as being one of the world's most eco-friendly breweries – collecting methane from waste-water treatment to use for power generation, augmenting wind power bought from Wyoming – New Belgium also gives every employee a new bike after a year's service, thus cutting down on staff travelling costs and pollution.

British Beer Exports

Country	'000 barrels
1 France	1299.9
2 USA	750.9
3 Ireland	579.8
4 Canada	194.4
5 Netherlands	108.0
6 Italy	75.9
7 Sweden	56.2
8 Spain	45.6
9 Belgium & Luxembourg	38.2
10 Australia	26.7
11 Japan	24.1
12 Germany	16.9
13 Denmark	11.4
14 Russian Federation	11.2
15 Greece	10.4
Other countries	102.5

Figures given are for 2009.

Source: British Beer & Pub Association Statistical Handbook 2010.

The Carter Legacy

Beer lovers have much to thank former US President Jimmy Carter for. It was Carter who signed into law the right to home brew in 1978, a move that led eventually to home brewers gaining experience, turning professional and establishing the remarkable craft brewing industry we witness today in the USA. Carter's brother, Billy, also left a legacy, although not such a glorious one. Noted as a fan of Pabst Blue Ribbon, Billy Carter was courted by Falls City Brewing of Kentucky, who were looking to establish a new brand bearing his name. The idea was to contract brew at breweries across the USA, so establishing a new national brand. Carter agreed and Billy Beer was born. It wasn't a success. Billy died in 1988 but the beer had disappeared long before.

Beer Writers of the Year

The British Guild of Beer Writers was founded in 1988 with the aim of improving the quality and quantity of writing about beer in the media. Its membership is open to book authors, print journalists, online writers, broadcasters, PR professionals, photographers and illustrators. The Guild presents the Beer Writer of the Year awards every December.

1988	Allan McLean	**2000**	Alastair Gilmour
1989	Michael Jackson	**2001**	Jeff Evans
1990	Allan McLean	**2002**	Michael Jackson
1991	Michael Hardman	**2003**	Martyn Cornell
1992	Allan McLean	**2004**	Ben McFarland
1993	Brian Glover	**2005**	Alastair Gilmour
1994	Roger Protz	**2006**	Ben McFarland
1995	Andrew Jefford	**2007**	Alastair Gilmour
1996	Michael Jackson	**2008**	Zak Avery
1997	Roger Protz	**2009**	Pete Brown
1998	Alastair Gilmour	**2010**	Simon Jenkins
1999	Andrew Jefford		

Vintage Ales

The wine world is anchored in the concept of vintage – the year in which a wine was produced. Beer also has its vintage products, beers that benefit from being set aside to mature in the bottle. The best known is Fuller's Vintage Ale, first produced in 1997 and released every autumn to great acclaim. The company has hosted comparative tastings of every year's release. Also from the UK comes Lees Harvest Ale. Again issued every autumn, this beer takes advantage of the latest barley and hop harvests. Year-dated, the beers are treasured by both collectors and those who wish to savour how the beer has aged. Sadly, no longer in production is Thomas Hardy's Ale, once brewed by Eldridge Pope and latterly by O'Hanlon's, and presented with a year-dated label. Better news concerns Gale's Prize Old Ale, also vintage dated and now being looked after by the brewers at Fuller's. In the USA, Alaskan Brewing date-marks its remarkable Smoked Porter and has allowed visitors to the Great American Beer Festival in Denver to sample various vintages.

Classic Carbonnade with Trappist Ale

Traditionally in Belgium, *carbonnade flamande* is made with one of the Flemish sour brown beers of East Flanders, but in her 1999 work *The Beer Cook Book* (published by Faber & Faber), Susan Nowak ventured into Trappist territory, adding a heavenly twist to this very popular dish.

Ingredients (serves six)

6 portions good braising steak
1 bottle Chimay Red
(just over 300 ml or 1/2 pint)
6 peppercorns
1 bay leaf
lard for frying
3 small red onions, sliced thinly
3 cloves garlic, crushed
2 rashers smoked fat streaky
bacon, diced
1 small celeriac, peeled and cubed

1 leek, cleaned and sliced
1 medium carrot, peeled and
sliced thinly
1 small raw beetroot, peeled and
cubed
1 tbsp tomato purée
1 heaped tbsp seasoned plain
flour
85 ml (3 fl oz) beef stock
1 bouquet garni
salt and pepper

Place steaks in a dish and pour over the Chimay Red, add peppercorns and bay leaf and marinate overnight. Next day fry onions, bacon and garlic in lard over a medium heat for around 30 seconds, then add celeriac, leek and carrot and fry for another two minutes, stirring, until lightly browned. Remove with a slotted spoon to the bottom of a heavy casserole dish.

Take steak from marinade, pat dry with kitchen paper and quickly brown on all sides in the fat left in the pan to seal in the beer, then place on top of the vegetables and put in the beetroot and tomato purée. Add a little more lard to the pan, if necessary, heat and sprinkle in the flour, stirring it in briskly and cooking for one to two minutes. Pour in the beef stock and bring slowly to simmering point while it thickens.

Remove from heat, stir in the rest of the marinade, pour over the steak in the casserole, add the bouquet garni, cover and cook very slowly towards the bottom of a low oven (325° F, 160° C, gas mark 3) for three hours, or until the meat is tender and the gravy slightly thickened. Taste and season if necessary (the beer adds a good deal of spiciness), remove the bay leaf and bouquet garni and serve with mashed potatoes and a green vegetable – Brussels sprouts, even!

Five Facts About Yeast

Yeast is a single-celled fungus that lives wild in the environment but is cultivated by brewers.

In ancient times, the scientific action of yeast was unknown to brewers. They didn't understand this strange substance in the atmosphere that fermented their beers and so they called it 'godisgood', after its divine benefits.

Brewers' yeast is a strain called *saccharomyces*, meaning sugar fungus. Ale yeasts fall into the group called *saccharomyces cerevisiae* and lager yeasts into the group called *saccharomyces uvarum*, *saccharomyces pastorianus* or *saccharomyces carlsbergensis*, the last after the Denmark brewery where it was cultivated.

As well as converting sugars into carbon dioxide and alcohol, yeast also imparts its own subtle flavours into the beer. This is why breweries maintain and protect their own strains of yeast.

Some brewers (particularly Belgian) also make use of a strain of yeast called *brettanomyces*. This converts yet more sugars to alcohol, creating a drier beer with distinct, earthy, rustic flavours.

Playing Hard to Get

Beers from the Westvleteren Trappist monastery brewery in Belgium are among the most difficult to source in the world. Such is the demand for their stunningly complex, potent ales that the monks ration their sales. If you want to buy some, you have to telephone the abbey at a given time (and no other: a schedule of what's available, and when, is posted on the abbey's website) and – assuming you actually get through – place an order. You will then be given a small allowance, if you're lucky, as long as you promise to keep it for personal consumption and not sell it on commercially. Alternatively, you can call into the abbey's own café (called In de Vrede), just across the road, where you can drink the beer, or perhaps even pick up a bottle or two to take away, but again you won't be able to load up the car (supplies to the café are also rationed).

A Slice of Pizza

In 2006, keen homebrewers Tom and Athena Seefurth stumbled upon an exciting new recipe. The Campton, Illinois, couple aimed to develop a beer to pair with their favourite food, pizza, and set to work with kitchen ingredients. The resultant Pizza Beer actually contains tomatoes, basil, oregano and garlic. It's now marketed as Mamma Mia! Pizza Beer.

Completely Organic British Breweries

Atlantic, Treisaac, Cornwall
Black Isle, Munlochy, Highland
Butts, Great Shefford, Berkshire
Little Valley, Hebden Bridge, West Yorkshire
Liverpool Organic, Liverpool, Merseyside
North Yorkshire, Pinchingthorpe, North Yorkshire
Pitfield, North Weald, Essex
Spectrum, Tharston, Norfolk

There are other breweries where much of the output is organic and plenty of others that produce at least one organic beer.

Dark Lord Day

The last Saturday in April is the time to head to Munster, Indiana, USA (close to Chicago). This is the day that the Three Floyds brewery releases the annual brew of its imperial Russian stout. Dark Lord (15% ABV) includes coffee and Mexican vanilla and has been dubbed by some the best beer in the world. Bottles are in such demand that they are only sold on this one day of the year, and only from the brewery itself. Dark Lord Day has turned into a celebration of craft beer, with around 6,000 beer lovers descending on the industrial park site. Dozens of beers from breweries other than Three Floyds are also on sale and live bands provide entertainment. Entrance is strictly by ticket only and tickets often exchange hands for many times the $10 face value. All ticket holders are guaranteed the chance to buy bottles of Dark Lord, but these are now limited to four per person, with even rarer wood-aged versions reserved for the winners of a scratch-off game on the tickets.

The Cyclist's Choice

When choosing a beer in Germany, beware of the one listed as Radler. This is the German equivalent of a shandy, a brewery-prepared mix of lager and lemonade, which is very popular, particularly among the country's many cyclists (*rad* = bike in German). On menus, it is usually listed as part of the brewery's beer range and many unaware tourists end up downing a shandy instead of a longed-for glass of German beer.

Beer Snacks Around the World

Pubs and bars in most countries tend to serve crisps (potato chips) and peanuts to their customers, but here are some of the most unusual offerings confronting drinkers as they order beers around the world (some snacks dished out free, others to be purchased at modest prices).

Belgium	Cubed cheese
Czech Republic	Pickled sausage, garlic bread, potato cakes
Eastern Europe	Fried garlic rye bread
Germany	Pretzels (soft), radishes, sausages
Japan	Boiled soya beans, dried fish, seaweed
Russia	Dried, salted fish, fried croutons, cheese
Spain	Tapas (various small plates of meat, fish, cheese, eggs or vegetables)
UK	Pork scratchings, pickled eggs, shellfish, pies
USA	Pretzels (hard), popcorn, beef jerky, nachos

Flip the Cap

Widely recognized as America's 'blue collar' beer, from its popularity among manual workers, Pabst Blue Ribbon hides a secret beneath each bottle cap. The inner lining of the cap carries a playing card symbol and a number, with different combinations in each bottle. PBR fans like to collect the full set or use the caps for drinking games. Some bars even offer the beer free if you can guess the combination in your bottle or if you score an ace. In a similar vein, Full Sail brewing in the USA hides 'rock, paper, scissors' symbols underneath the caps of its Session range.

Units of Alcohol

The UK Government advises that male drinkers should not regularly drink more than 3–4 units of alcohol per day, and women 2–3 units per day. However, there are a number of important provisos to these guidelines. For example, pregnant women and people with certain health conditions, or on some kinds of medication, should observe much lower limits, or abstain altogether.

A unit is a measure of 10 ml of pure alcohol. In the UK, these units are increasingly being shown on containers. However, where this is not the case, for example when you buy a pint of beer in a pub, you can work out how many units are in it for yourself, using the following formula:

Volume in millilitres (ml) x % alcohol by volume (ABV)
then divide by 1000

A pint is equivalent to 568 ml. So to find the units in a pint of beer at 3.5% ABV, multiply 568 x 3.5, then divide by 1000 = 1.988 units. A pint of beer at 5% ABV is 568 x 5 divided by 1000 = 2.84 units. Note, however that other countries have different values for units. For more information, check out the website of The Portman Group, an industry-sponsored body dedicated to responsible drinking, at www.portmangroup.org.uk.

Beers to Mature

Most beers benefit from being drunk young but some beers are well worth setting aside to see how the flavours ripen and mature over the course of months, if not years. Here are some beers to experiment with:

Alaskan Smoked Porter
Anchor Old Foghorn
Brooklyn Black Chocolate Stout
Chimay Grand Réserve
Coopers Vintage Ale
Dogfish Head Worldwide Stout
Durham Temptation
Fuller's Vintage Ale
Gale's Prize Old Ale

Harveys Imperial Extra Double Stout
La Trappe Quadrupel
Lees Harvest Ale
Meantime Porter
Orval
Pitfield 1896 XXXX Stock Ale
Rochefort 10
Sierra Nevada Bigfoot
Westvleteren 12

The Origins of Beer Names

1698 (Shepherd Neame) Date of founding of brewery

1845 (Fuller's) Date of founding of Fuller, Smith and Turner company

Angelus (Annoeuillin) Jean François Millet painting

Barbus Barbus (Butts) Latin name for the barbel fish

Bigfoot (Sierra Nevada) Mythical Californian 'missing link'

Black Douglas (Broughton) Sir James Douglas, 14th-century fighter for Scottish independence

Black Prince (St Austell) Edward, 14th-century Prince of Wales

Bluebird Bitter (Coniston) Donald Campbell's land and water speed machines

Bodgers Barley Wine (Chiltern) A local craftsman/ chairmaker

Chalky's Bite (Sharp's) TV Chef Rick Stein's Jack Russell terrier

Clouded Yellow (St Austell) Continental butterfly

Crack Shot (Daleside) 'Trooper' Jane Ingilby, English Civil War Royalist

Cross Buttock (Jennings) Cumbrian wrestling throw

Dark Lord (Batemans) Thomas Fairfax, English Civil War officer

Directors Bitter (Scottish Courage) Beer reserved for Courage board

Doff Cocker (Three Bs) Person who removed waste from the shuttle in a weaving machine

Doom Bar (Sharp's) Sandbank off Cornish coast

Double Header (RCH) Two-engined steam train

Edmund Fitzgerald Porter (Great Lakes) Freighter wrecked on Lake Superior in 1975

Elsie Mo (Castle Rock) Low Colour Maris Otter (LCMO) malt

Flying Shuttle (Thwaites) Revolutionary weaving device invented by John Kay in 1733

Gavroche (St-Sylvestre) Character in *Les Misérables*

Gonzo Imperial Porter (Flying Dog) Hunter S Thompson's 'gonzo' journalism

Good King Henry Special Reserve (Old Chimneys) Vegetable

Gouden Carolus (Het Anker) Gold coin minted during rule of Holy Roman Emperor Charles V

Great Cockup Porter (Hesket Newmarket) Cumbrian fell

Heart of Oak (Oakleaf) Naval marching tune

Hemlock (Castle Rock) Ancient rock formation near Nottingham

Humpty Dumpty (Humpty Dumpty) Class of steam locomotive

JHB (Oakham) Jeffrey Hudson, court midget of King Charles I

Kiss (Harveys) Sculpture by Auguste Rodin

The Leveller (Springhead) Radical, reforming Parliamentarian group during English Civil War

Leviathan (Hopdaemon) Biblical sea monster

Liberty Ale (Anchor) Paul Revere's ride during US War of Independence

Melton Red (Belvoir) Marquis of Waterford 'painting the town (Melton Mowbray) red' in 1837

Monkman's Slaughter (Cropton) Colin Monkman and Colin Slaughter, barley farmer and head brewer

Old Freddy Walker (Moor) Veteran mariner in the brewery's village

Old Horny (Blythe) Abbots Bromley annual Horn Dance

Old Peculier (Theakston's) The ecclesiastical court, or 'Peculier', of Masham

Old Speckled Hen (Greene King) A type of MG motorcar

Old Tom (Robinson's) Brewery cat

Pendle Witches Brew (Moorhouse's) Lancashire witch trials of 1612

Pitchfork (RCH) Pitchfork Rebellion of 1685

Postman's Knock (Hobsons) Postman/writer Simon Evans

Proper Job (St Austell) Sterling effort by Cornish soldiers during Indian Mutiny of 1857

Proud Salopian (Salopian) Thomas Southam, the 'Proud Salopian' brewer

Red MacGregor (Orkney) Rob Roy, 17th-century Scottish brigand

Riggwelter (Black Sheep) Term for a sheep on its back, struggling to get up

Roaring Meg (Springhead) English Civil War cannon

Shropshire Lad (Wood) AE Housman poem

Side Pocket for a Toad (Tring) Colloquialism for something useless

Skull Splitter (Orkney) Thorfinn Einarsson, 7th Viking Earl of Orkney

Spingo (Blue Anchor) From 'stingo', an old name for strong beer

Summer Lightning (Hop Back) PG Wodehouse novel

Trafalgar (Freeminer) Forest of Dean coal-mine

Umbel Ale (Nethergate) The flowers of coriander, an ingredient, have an umbel (botanic term) shape

Victory Ale (Batemans) Celebration of saving brewery's independence

Waggle Dance (Young's) Movement of bees pointing out source of nectar (a honey beer)

Wherry (Woodforde's) Type of Norfolk Broads sailing boat

Workie Ticket (Mordue) Geordie term for a loafer

Salvator 'Clones'

Acknowledged as the first ever doppelbock is a beer from the Paulaner brewery in Munich. This strong lager (7.5% ABV) was reportedly first brewed by monks, to keep them fortified during Lent, when solid foods were banned. It eventually went on public sale under the name Salvator ('Saviour'), which Paulaner trade-marked in 1896. However, this didn't stop rival breweries making their own beers in the same style. They even referred to the original by adding the suffix 'ator' to the names of their beers, a practice now copied around the world, particularly in the USA, where an element of fun has been introduced. Here are some examples.

Germany

Brewery	Beer	Brewery	Beer
Allgäuer	Cambonator	Kulmbacher	Kulminator
Augustiner	Maximator	Löwenbräu	Triumphator
Ayinger	Celebrator	Maxlrainer	Jubilator
Eichhofener	Eichator	Prösslbräu	Palmator
Hacker-Pschorr	Animator	Riegele	Speziator
Hutthurmer	Kulinator	Spaten	Optimator
Kaufbeuren	Buronator	Tucher	Bajuvator

USA

Brewery	Beer	Brewery	Beer
Ballast Point	Navigator	HeBrew	Rejewvenator
Bells	Consecrator	Iron Hill	Ironator
Breakwater	Devastator	Sixpoint	Emasculator
Church Brew	Paganator	Sly Fox	Instigator
Dock Street	Illuminator	Smuttynose	Smuttonator
Elevator	Procrastinator	Stoudt	Smooth Hoperator
Fish Tale	Detonator	Thomas Hooker	Liberator
Flying Dog	Collaborator	Tröegs	Troegenator
Goose Island	Aviator	Two Brothers	Incinerator

The Chemical Equation for Fermentation

$$C_6H_{12}O_6 \longrightarrow 2(CH_3CH_2OH) + 2(CO_2)$$

(glucose)   (ethyl alcohol)   (carbon dioxide)

Rodent Ale

'The Rat, meanwhile, was busy examining the label on one of the beer-bottles. "I perceive this to be Old Burton," he remarked approvingly. "Sensible Mole! The very thing! Now we shall be able to mull some ale!"'

The Wind in the Willows, Kenneth Grahame

Television's Fictional Beers and Breweries

Beer/Brewery	Programme
Alamo Beer	King of the Hill
Benderbrau	Futurama
Causton Ales	Midsomer Murders
Chapston's	Where the Heart Is
Dharma Beer	Lost
Duff Beer	The Simpsons
Ephraim Monk	Emmerdale
Heisler Beer	Various US series
Luxford & Copley	EastEnders
Newton & Ridley	Coronation Street
Pawtucket Patriot Ale	Family Guy
Shotz	Laverne & Shirley

The Land of Lambic

The wine industry places much importance on terroir – the combination of land and climate that dictates the character of the product. In beer, terroir exists but is not so well defined. However, it is very clearly expressed in the survival of a handful of breweries and beer blenders in an area of Belgium. Payottenland is a rural region to the south and west of Brussels. It is home to the lambic style of beer, the beer that is famously fermented using wild yeasts that survive in the atmosphere. Brewers around the world attempt their own versions of these idiosyncratic beers but the yeasts and other local bacteria are so important to the character of the beer that only in Payottenland, and in neighbouring parts of Brussels itself, can real lambic ever be produced.

CAMRA's Champion Beers of Britain

The Campaign for Real Ale's Champion Beer of Britain contest is judged on the first day of the Great British Beer Festival each summer. It is the UK's most prestigious cask ale competition, with all beers judged in categories, before an overall winner is elected. Here are the champions to date. Brewers' records in the competition are listed on pages 52–3.

1978	Thwaites Best Mild/ Fuller's ESB	**1995**	Cottage Norman's Conquest
1979	Fuller's London Pride	**1996**	Woodforde's Wherry
1980	Thwaites Best Mild	**1997**	Mordue Workie Ticket
1981	Fuller's ESB	**1998**	Coniston Bluebird Bitter
1982	Taylor Landlord	**1999**	Taylor Landlord
1983	Taylor Landlord	**2000**	Moorhouse's Black Cat Mild
1984	No event	**2001**	Oakham JHB
1985	Fuller's ESB	**2002**	Caledonian Deuchars IPA
1986	Batemans XXXB	**2003**	Harviestoun Bitter & Twisted
1987	Pitfield Dark Star	**2004**	Kelham Island Pale Rider
1988	Ringwood Old Thumper	**2005**	Crouch Vale Brewers Gold
1989	Fuller's Chiswick Bitter	**2006**	Crouch Vale Brewers Gold
1990	Ind Coope Burton Ale	**2007**	Hobsons Mild
1991	Mauldons Black Adder	**2008**	Triple fff Alton's Pride
1992	Woodforde's Norfolk Nog	**2009**	Rudgate Ruby Mild
1993	Adnams Extra	**2010**	Castle Rock Harvest Pale
1994	Taylor Landlord	**2011**	Mighty Oak Oscar Wilde

Starkbierzeit

The Germans need little excuse for a beery knees-up and one of the biggest takes place in Munich each year. No: we're not talking about the Oktoberfest. The event in question is the Starkbierzeit (literally 'strong beer time'), a chance to indulge in the drinking of some seriously strong lager. The festivities, beginning on St Joseph's Day (19 March), mark the end of winter and kick off with the official, high-profile tapping of a cask of Paulaner Salvator, the 7.5% doppelbock that was once brewed only for consumption by monks. The strong beer celebration continues for a couple of weeks, as other breweries and associated pubs join in the fun.

CAMRA's Champion Winter Beers of Britain

Beers in the categories of Strong Milds/Old Ales, Stouts/Porters and Barley Wines have been judged separately from the Champion Beer of Britain contest since 1996/7, with the overall winner declared Champion Winter Beer of Britain. These are the supreme winter champions to date.

Winter 1996/7	Hambleton Nightmare
Winter 1997/8	Nethergate Old Growler
1999	Dent T'Owd Tup
2000	Robinson's Old Tom
2001	Orkney Skull Splitter
2002	Wye Valley Dorothy Goodbody's Wholesome Stout
2003	Nethergate Old Growler
2004	Moor Old Freddy Walker
2005	Robinson's Old Tom
2006	Hogs Back A over T
2007	Green Jack Ripper
2008	Wickwar Station Porter
2009	Oakham Attila
2010	Elland 1872 Porter
2011	Hop Back Entire Stout

Houblon and Orge Days

One of the benefits brought about by the French Revolution was the recognition of the value of hops and barley to the ordinary man. The new regime achieved this by installing a replacement calendar, casting aside the former religious date system, with its saints' days, and introducing one based on what the revolutionaries believed really mattered to the working man. Months were renamed after the weather or what they contributed to life, and days were dedicated to tools, plants, animals and other things intrinsic to the daily grind. Alongside other crops, hops and barley were honoured with their own days. Houblon, or hops, were cherished on the 23rd day of Fructidor ('Fruit'), while orge, or barley, was celebrated on the 29th day of Vendémiaire ('Vintage'). If you'd like to celebrate them today, the dates translate in the modern calendar as 9 September and 20 October, respectively.

Imperial Beer Measurements

Barrel .... 36 gallons
Gallon .... 8 pints
Quart .... 2 pints (40 fluid ounces)
Pint .... 20 fluid ounces
Nip .... $^1/_3$ pint
Gill .... 5 fluid ounces ($^1/_4$ pint)
Yard of Ale .... $2^1/_4$–$4^1/_2$ pints (not standard)

US Beer Measurements

Barrel .... 31 gallons
Gallon .... 8 pints
Quart .... 2 pints (32 fluid ounces)
Pint .... 16 fluid ounces

International Bittering Units

Sometimes beers are described as having so many 'units of bitterness'. This is a figure based on the amount of alpha acid (the bittering component of the hop) there is in a beer. One International Bitterness Unit (IBU) is equivalent to 1 mg of alpha acid per 1 litre of beer. The lower the bitterness unit figure, the less bitter the beer is likely to be. Some typical IBUs for beer styles, in increasing levels of bitterness, are:

American light lager	10	Tripel	30
Lambic	15	US pale ale	35
Weissbier	15	Pilsner	35
Dunkel	20	Stout	35
Helles	20	Barley wine	40
Mild	20	IPA	45
Witbier	20	Imperial stout	50
Bock	25	US imperial stout	50+
Dubbel	25	US IPA	50+
Bitter	30	US barley wine	60+
Porter	30	Imperial/double IPA	65+

Barley Town-upon-Tweed

Widely known for being England's most northerly town and for having the only football team in England to play in the Scottish League (Berwick Rangers), Berwick-upon-Tweed also has a significance for beer lovers. 'Berwick' is actually an old English word meaning 'barley town'.

The Top 20 Beer-Drinking Nations

	Country	Litres per head		Country	Litres per head
1	Czech Republic	154.1	11	Denmark	85.8
2	Ireland	117.4	12	Australia	84.0
3	Germany	111.1	13	UK	83.5
4	Austria	109.7	14	Croatia	83.3
5	Romania	99.0	15	USA	82.3
6	Slovenia	94.8	16	Belgium & Luxembourg	82.0
7	Poland	90.1	17	Russian Federation	81.0
8	Finland	89.6	18	New Zealand	78.9
	Lithuania	89.6	19	Spain	78.2
10	Venezuela	88.7	20	Slovakia	77.3

Figures show annual beer consumption in 2008.

Source: British Beer & Pub Association Statistical Handbook 2010.

The British Yeast

There is a strain of yeast commonly associated with the spontaneously fermented lambic beers of Belgium. It is a wild yeast that lives in the atmosphere and adds its own flavour profile to the brew, resulting – when combined with the effects of other yeasts and friendly bacteria – in an earthy, leathery, rustic taste. The yeast is known as *brettanomyces*, literally meaning British yeast. Its name is indicative of just how little control British (and, to be fair, other) brewers once exerted over their beers. Subject to wild yeast strains pervading the brewhouse, British ales would be infected with *brettanomyces* and produce these strange 'off' flavours. The phenomenon was recognized at the turn of the 20th century by Danish brewer/scientist Niels Hjelte Claussen, who bestowed the British title on this influential, and now much cherished, fungus.

The Michelin Stars

Most restaurants present an excellent range of wines, but few offer any decent choice of beer. Even among Michelin-starred establishments, the beer on the menu may just boil down to a bottle of bland international lager. Imagine if their wine lists just consisted of Blue Nun and Jacob's Creek! There are some notable exceptions, however, including the following British Michelin-starred restaurants, where beer is treated seriously and properly, and given the respect it deserves.

> **Kinloch Lodge**, Isle of Skye
> **Le Gavroche**, London
> **Le Manoir aux Quat' Saisons**, Oxfordshire
> **Quilon**, London

The Brewer Governor

John Hickenlooper's story proves yet again that beer has the power to change society. In the 1980s, Hickenlooper, a former oil industry worker, recognized an opportunity to open a brewpub (the first in Colorado) in a derelict warehouse in Denver's LoDo (lower downtown) district. The area, close to the railroad station, did not have a good reputation and there were some who feared that Hickenlooper's project might only make things worse. Instead, Hickenlooper's foresight in creating the enormous Wynkoop pub and brewery was handsomely rewarded, not only in ringing cash tills but also in the uplift it gave to LoDo. Soon other entrepreneurs moved in to turn the district's run-down buildings into art galleries, restaurants and sought-after apartments. Even the Colorado Rockies, Denver's baseball team, moved their ballpark to within a few blocks of the Wynkoop, with Coors brewery opening its own brewpub inside it. Not surprisingly, the ever-enthusiastic, engaging Hickenlooper became a popular figure and was urged to run for high office. Standing as an independent, he scored a landslide victory over seven other candidates and a good time was enjoyed by the Wynkoop's regulars that exciting evening in July 2003 when John was sworn in as the 43rd Mayor of Denver. In 2010, Hickenlooper's star rose even higher when he was elected Governor of Colorado on the Democratic ticket. Mayor, Governor ... could we soon have a brewer in The White House?

Chain Pub Ownership

Chain	Owner
All Bar One	Mitchells & Butlers
Beefeater	Whitbread
Brewers Fayre	Whitbread
Chef & Brewer	Spirit
Crown Carveries	Mitchells & Butlers
Ember Inns	Mitchells & Butlers
Fayre & Square	Spirit
Flaming Grill	Spirit
Good Night Inns	Spirit
Harvester	Mitchells & Butlers
Hog's Head	Stonegate
Hungry Horse	Greene King
Innkeeper's Lodge	Mitchells & Butlers
John Barras	Spirit
Lloyds No.1	Wetherspoon
Nicholson's	Mitchells & Butlers
O'Neill's	Mitchells & Butlers
Old English Inns	Greene King
Original Pub Company	Spirit
Pitcher & Piano	Marston's
Premier Inns	Whitbread
Real Local Pubs	Spirit
Roast Inn	Spirit
Scream	Stonegate
Sizzling Pubs	Mitchells & Butlers
Slug & Lettuce	Stonegate
Smith & Jones	Barracuda
Table Table	Whitbread
Taylor Walker	Spirit
Toby Pub & Carvery	Mitchells & Butlers
Varsity	Barracuda
Village Pub & Kitchen	Mitchells & Butlers
Vintage Inn	Mitchells & Butlers
Wacky Warehouse	Spirit
Walkabout	Intertain
Yates's	Stonegate

Beer and Food Pairing: An Elementary List

Wine makes a fine companion at dinner time, we all know that. But so does beer. In fact, when you consider the huge variety of flavours beer can bring to a meal – anything from zesty citrus notes, through caramel, nut and tropical fruits, to deep, rich chocolate and coffee – it is scandalous that our favourite tipple has been kept off the fine dining table for so long. Now, however, increasing numbers of chefs – from those working in pubs and bars to those running high-end restaurants – are recognizing just how perfect a partner beer can be for food. There is a beer available to match every type of food, with flavours to enhance the nuances of the dish, as this elementary food pairing table suggests.

Before Dining

Aperitifs	Pilsners; hoppy bitters; Belgian wheat beers; Belgian fruit beers

Starters

Fish	German lagers; golden ales; Belgian wheat beers
Pasta	Tomato sauce – amber ales; Vienna lagers
	Cream sauce – Bavarian wheat beers
	Pesto – hoppy bitters; pilsners; tripels
Pâté	Milds; dunkels; Trappist ales
Quiches/soufflés	Wheat beers
Risotto	Bavarian wheat beers; tripels
Shellfish	Stouts; porters; Belgian wheat beers
Soups	Vegetable – golden ales
	Meaty – brown ales

Main Courses

Barbecue	Smoked beers; dunkels; brown ales
Beef	Bitters; Trappist ales
Chicken	Vienna lagers; wheat beers
Curries	IPAs; strong lagers
Duck	Belgian fruit beers; Trappist ales
Gammon	Smoked beers; pilsners
Goose	Belgian brown ales
Lamb	Brown ales; dunkels; bières de garde
Liver	Belgian brown ales

Meat pies	Strong bitters; brown ales; Trappist ales
Mexican	Vienna lagers; American pale ales
Oriental	Wheat beers; ginger/spiced beers
Pheasant	Brown ales; Belgian brown ales
Pizzas	Vienna lagers; amber ales
Ploughman's	Fruity bitters
Pork	Pilsners; Bavarian wheat beers; dunkels
Sausages	Strong bitters; dunkels
Turkey	Brown ales; Belgian brown ales
Venison	Trappist ales; Belgian fruit beers

Vegetables

Asparagus	Tripels
Avocado	American pale ales
Lentils	Brown ales; dunkels
Mushrooms	Brown ales; dunkels
Nuts	Brown ales; dunkels
Peas	Bavarian wheat beers
Salads	Floral bitters; wheat beers
Spinach	Bavarian wheat beers
Sweetcorn	Helles lagers; Bavarian wheat beers

Cheeses

Goat's	Belgian fruit beers; wheat beers
Mature/Blue	Trappist ales; old ales; barley wines; IPAs
Mild	Golden ales; wheat beers
Strong	Strong ales; brown ales

Desserts

Apple/banana	Bavarian wheat beers
Cheesecake	Belgian fruit beers; sweet stouts; imperial stouts
Chocolate/coffee	Porters; stouts; Belgian fruit beers
Creamy	Stouts
Fruit cake	Barley wines
Fruit tarts	Stouts
Ice Cream	Barley wines; sweet stouts; imperial stouts; Belgian fruit beers
Red berry	Porters
Spiced	Bavarian wheat beers

Beer Drinkers of the Year (UK)

The 'Beer Drinker of the Year' award is presented by the All-Party Parliamentary Beer Group to the person who, in the opinion of the judges, has made a signal contribution to British life, with special reference to beer, during the previous year. Here are the winners to date.

1994   Rt. Hon. Kenneth Clarke QC MP (Chancellor of the Exchequer)
1995   Jack Charlton OBE (football manager)
1996   Anna Chancellor (actress)
1997   John Lowe OBE (darts player)
1998   John Cryne (retiring Chairman of CAMRA)
1999   Michael Parkinson OBE (journalist and talk show host)
2000   Edward Kelsey (aka 'Joe Grundy' of Radio 4's *The Archers*)
2001   Darren Gough (cricketer)
2002   HRH The Prince of Wales
2003   Nigel Jones MP (retiring Chairman of the All-Party
             Parliamentary Beer Group)
2004   Roger Protz (Editor, *Good Beer Guide*, and beer writer)
2005   Rt. Hon. Gordon Brown MP (Chancellor of the Exchequer)
2006   Andrew Flintoff (cricketer)
2007   Michel Roux (chef)
2008   Nick Hewer (PR consultant/TV personality)
2009   David and Robert Aynesworth (publicans)
2010   John Grogan (past Chairman of the All-Party Parliamentary
             Beer Group)
2011   Sriram Aylur (chef)

UK Breweries Still Using Dray Horses for Deliveries

In the days before motorized transport, horses were a familiar sight pulling the drays that delivered beer to pubs. Now just a trio of breweries still maintain a team of these gentle giants – not because they are economical, but because the public relations value is enormous, emphasizing tradition. Listed below are the three British breweries still employing these environmentally-friendly horses for regular deliveries.

Hook Norton   Samuel Smith   Wadworth

Beer Drinkers of the Year (US)

America's 'Beer Drinker of the Year' is discovered in a challenging contest held at The Wynkoop brewpub in Denver. The winner is selected on the basis of his/her 'beer resumé' and after close scrutiny by a panel of robed and bewigged expert judges, who fire a selection of questions designed to test the candidates' knowledge of beer, wit and ingenuity.

1997 Jack McDougall, Cranford, New Jersey
1998 Bobby Bush, Jr., Hickory, North Carolina
1999 James Robertson, Pomona, California
2000 Steve Pawlowski, Roselle Park, New Jersey
2001 Cornelia Corey, Clemmons, North Carolina
2002 Gary Steinel, White Plains, New York
2003 Ray McCoy, Clemmons, North Carolina
2004 John Marioni, Seattle, Washington
2005 Tom Ciccateri, Alexandria, Virginia
2006 Tom Schmidlin, Seattle, Washington
2007 Diane Catanzaro, Norfolk, Virginia
2008 Matt Venzke, Yorktown, Virginia
2009 Cody Christman, Golden, Colorado
2010 Bill Howell, Sterling, Alaska
2011 Phil Farrell, Cumming, Georgia

American Craft Brewing Redefined

In 2011, the Brewers Association revised its definition of what constitutes a 'craft brewer' in the USA to reflect the remarkable growth in the craft brewing sector and the success of some of its largest members. According to the new parameters, an American craft brewer is small, independent and traditional. 'Small' restricts annual production to 6 million US barrels or less (up from a cap of 2 million barrels). 'Independent' means that less than 25% of the brewery is owned or controlled by an alcoholic beverage producer that is not itself a craft brewer. 'Traditional' dictates that the brewer either has an all-malt flagship brew (the beer which represents the greatest volume among its brands) or at least 50% of its output is devoted to all-malt beers or beers that use adjuncts only to enhance, rather than lighten, flavour.

Ten Collectors' Societies

1   **American Breweriana Association** (ABA)
    Established in 1982; now has nearly 3,000 members in the USA
    and around the world. www.americanbreweriana.org

2   **Association for British Brewery Collectables** (ABBC)
    Founded in 1983 as the Association of Bottled Beer Collectors,
    now covering all UK breweriana. www.breweriana.org.uk

3   **Australian Beer Can Collectors' Association** (ABCCA)
    Founded in 1979. www.abcca.com.au

4   **Brewery Collectibles Club of America** (BCCA)
    Founded in 1970 as Beer Can Collectors of America, an
    organisation covering all items of breweriana. www.bcca.com

5   **British Beer Can Collectors' Society**
    Society founded in 1978 as Wessex Beer Can Collectors' Society.

6   **British Beermat Collectors' Society**
    The organisation for tegestologists, founded in 1960, with
    comedians Morecambe and Wise as the first presidents.

7   **British Brewery Playing Card Society** (BBPCS)
    Society for collectors of single cards and packs issued by
    breweries, bottlers and cidermakers. www.bbpcs.co.uk

8   **The Guinness Collectors' Club**
    Devoted to collectors of all kinds of Guinness memorabilia, from
    ash trays to Corgi toys. www.guinntiques.com

9   **The Labologists' Society**
    Founded by Guinness in 1958, now an independent society for
    collectors of beer labels. www.labology.org.uk

10 **National Association of Breweriana Advertising** (NABA)
    Set up in 1972 to promote the preservation of US brewery
    advertising material. www.nababrew.com

The World's Biggest Beer Markets

Country	Million US Barrels		Country	Million US Barrels
1 China	368.1	6	Mexico	55.2
2 USA	202.1	7	Japan	51.0
3 Brazil	89.1	8	UK	43.0
4 Russia	84.8	9	Spain	27.8
5 Germany	76.6	10	Poland	27.5

Figures given are for 2009. Source: Impact Databank.

CAMRA's National Pubs of the Year

1988	The Boar's Head, Kinmuck, Aberdeenshire
1989	The Cap & Feathers, Tillingham, Essex
1990	The Bell, Aldworth, Berkshire
1991	The Great Western, Wolverhampton, West Midlands
1992	No award*
1993	The Three Kings Inn, Hanley Castle, Worcestershire / The Fisherman's Tavern, Broughty Ferry, Perth & Kinross
1994	The Beamish Mary Inn, No Place, County Durham
1995	The Coalbrookedale Inn, Coalbrookedale, Shropshire
1996	The Halfway House, Pitney, Somerset
1997	The Sair Inn, Linthwaite, West Yorkshire
1997/8	The Volunteer Arms (Staggs), Musselburgh, Midlothian*
1998	The Fat Cat, Norwich, Norfolk
1999	The Rising Sun, Tipton, West Midlands
2000	The Blisland Inn, Blisland, Cornwall
2001	The Nursery, Heaton Norris, Greater Manchester
2002	The Swan, Little Totham, Essex
2003	The Crown & Thistle, Gravesend, Kent
2004	The Fat Cat, Norwich, Norfolk
2005	The Swan, Little Totham, Essex
2006	The Tom Cobley Tavern, Spreyton, Devon
2007	The Old Spot Inn, Dursley, Gloucestershire
2008	Kelham Island Tavern, Sheffield
2009	Kelham Island Tavern, Sheffield
2010	The Harp, Covent Garden, London

*Awards have been made at various times of the year, hence the peculiar dating.

Britain's 'Big Six' National Breweries When CAMRA Was Founded

Allied Breweries   Scottish & Newcastle
Bass Charrington   Watney
Courage   Whitbread

Britain's 'Big Four' International Breweries Today

A-B InBev UK (ultimately the owner of Whitbread and some of Bass)
Carlsberg UK (ultimately the owner of what was Allied Breweries)
Heineken UK (ultimately the owner of Scottish & Newcastle and Watney)
Molson Coors (ultimately the owner of much of Bass)

Former 'Big Six' brewer Courage's brands are now owned by Wells & Young's.

Major US Brewpub Chains

Brewpubs were once commonplace in the US, but died out during Prohibition. After changes in state laws in the 1980s, the concept was revived and now brewpubs blossom all across the country. Many are single, independently-owned outlets but a number belong to national or regional chains. In terms of beer sales, these are the top ten chains.

	Brewpub Chain	Outlets*
1	CraftWorks Restaurants and Breweries**	70
2	Granite City Brewing Co	26
3	McMenamin's Breweries	24
4	RAM/Big Horn Brewery	20
5	BJ's Restaurant and Brewery	16
6	Iron Hill Brewery & Restaurant	8
7	Oggi's Pizza & Brewing Co	7
8	Karl Strauss Brewing Co	6
9	John Harvard's Brew House	5
10	Back Street Brewery	5

*Excludes non-brewing restaurants.

**Parent company of the Rock Bottom and Gordon Biersch chains.

Figures given are for 2010. Source: Brewers Association.

Common Faults in Bottled Beer

Beers that are not well brewed can exhibit significant off flavours. The problems can be even worse in bottled beers that have not been well packaged and/or stored. Here is a list of common faults and causes.

Taste/Smell	Fault	Reason
Butterscotch	Diacetyl	Inadequate fermentation/conditioning
Cheese	Isovaleric Acid	Stale hops or bacterial infection
Disinfectant/TCP	Chlorophenol	Yeast problems/chlorine cleaning residue
Farmyard	4-Ethyl Phenol	Wild yeast infection (possibly deliberate)
Green apples	Acetaldehyde	Young beer
Marmite/soy sauce	Autolysis	Breakdown of yeast cells
Rotten eggs	Hydrogen Sulphide	Yeast by-product, mostly in young beer
Skunky	Mercaptans	Lightstrike: light reacting with chemicals in hops
Sweetcorn/ vegetables	DMS	Dimethyl Sulphide: inadequate boil
Wet paper	Trans 2-Nonenal	Oxidation: oxygen reacting with beer

The Structure of a Traditional Wooden Cask

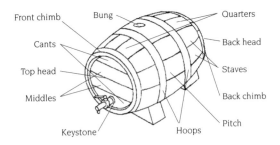

Front chimb · Bung · Quarters · Cants · Back head · Top head · Staves · Middles · Back chimb · Keystone · Hoops · Pitch

Menu Prepared by Sriram Aylur for the Annual Dinner of the British Guild of Beer Writers 2010

Papadoms with Coriander Chutney
served with
Jever Pilsener

* * *

Crab Cakes with Soya Bean Chop
served with
Goose Island 312 Urban Wheat Ale

* * *

Black Cod with Quilon Salad
served with
Chimay Red

* * *

Lamb Biryani with Spinach Porial
served with
Badger Blandford Fly

* * *

Bibinca
served with
Brooklyn Black Chocolate Stout

Sriram Aylur – the All Party Parliamentary Beer Group's 'Beer Drinker of the Year 2011' – is the Michelin-starred chef from Quilon restaurant, Victoria, London, which specializes in the cuisine of India's south-western coast.

The Price of Your Pint

This table below highlights beer price increases in the UK versus those of other daily commodities since the time CAMRA was founded in 1971.

Item	1971 Price	2011 Price	% Increase
Pint of Milk	5p	45p	900%
Pound of Rump Steak	60p	522p	870%
Sliced Loaf	9.5p	100p	1052%
Pint of Beer	12p	284p*	2366%

*Average price of a pint of cask-conditioned ale before the 2011 Budget duty increase.

Brewery Revivals

Rather than adopt a fresh name, a number of newly-established British breweries have set out to revive the name of a brewery that closed some years, if not decades, earlier. Here are some examples of such revivals.

Name	Location	Original Closure	Re-Established
Brampton	Chesterfield	1955	2007
Cain's	Liverpool	1923	1991
Ilkley	Ilkley	1923	2009
Joule's	Market Drayton*	1974	2010
Lovibonds	Henley-on-Thames**	1959	2005
Mauldons	Sudbury	1960	1981
Nailsworth	Nailsworth	1908	2004
Nottingham	Nottingham	1952	2001
Rhymney	Merthyr Tydfil***	1978	2005
Truman's****	London	1989	2010

*Original location was Stone.

**Main brewery was at Greenwich.

***Original location was Rhymney.

****Beers currently brewed under contract.

Beer Heroes: Pierre Celis (1925–2011)

The popularity of Belgian witbiers can be laid at the door of one man. It was dairyman Pierre Celis who revived the style in the 1960s, having helped out as a youth at a brewery that produced such a beer. He set up his own brewhouse in the town of Hoegaarden and reproduced the cloudy, spiced wheat beer that locals loved but had lost. After early success, Celis sold the brewery to Interbrew, which took the beer onto a world stage, hotly followed by other multi-nationals, once they had discovered similar wheat beers from the Low Countries, like Brugs Tarwebier, Gulpener Korenwolf and Wieckse Witte. Celis emigrated to Texas where he developed the style for the American market with similar success. The Celis White he brewed in Austin led to plenty of copies and was eventually bought by Miller, which, bizarrely, closed the Texas brewery. Celis White survives its creator. It is now brewed by Michigan Brewery in the USA, and by Van Steenberge in Celis's native Belgium.

JD Wetherspoon Pubs Named After Famous People

Pub chain operator JD Wetherspoon has named many of its pubs after dignitaries and achievers. Some are only well known locally but here is a list of some of the more famous people celebrated around the UK.

Pub Name	Location	Reason
Admiral Byng	Potters Bar	Executed naval officer lived nearby
Alexander Graham Bell	Edinburgh	Telephone pioneer born in city
Amy Johnson	Doncaster	Aviator honoured in Robin Hood Airport pub
Aneurin Bevan	Cardiff	Welsh father of the National Health Service
Edmund Halley	Lee Green	Comet discoverer buried in local churchyard
Eric Bartholomew	Morecambe	Comedian Eric (Morecambe) born in town
Claude du Vall	Camberley	Notorious highwayman 'worked' nearby
Gary Cooper	Dunstable	Actor attended local school
Hedley Verity	Leeds	Cricketer born and played locally
Henry Bessemer	Workington	Steel pioneer worked in town
Herbert Wells	Woking	Author (HG Wells) lived in town
Isaac Pitman	Trowbridge	Shorthand pioneer born in town
Isambard Kingdom Brunel	Portsmouth	Engineer born in the city
James Watt	Greenock	Inventor/engineer born in town
John Logie Baird	Hastings	Pioneered television experiments in town
John Masefield	New Ferry	Poet Laureate lived in town
Joseph Bramah	Barnsley	WC and handpump inventor born in town
King James	Cheshunt	King had palace nearby
Lord Wilson	Huddersfield	Prime Minister (Harold Wilson) born in town
Mary Shelley	Bournemouth	Author buried in town
Percy Florence Shelley	Boscombe	Son of famous poet lived nearby

Perkin Warbeck	Taunton	Pretender to throne imprisoned in town
Prince Arthur	Fleet	Victoria's son was CO of local army camp
Reginald Mitchell	Hanley	Spitfire designer attended local school
Richmal Crompton	Bromley	Author lived, and was a teacher, in town
Robert Peel	Bury	Local MP, father of Prime Minister of same name
Robert the Bruce	Dumfries	Scottish king murdered rival at local monastery
Rohan Kanhai	Ashington	West Indies cricketer played for local club
Rupert Brooke	Rugby	War poet born in town
Sir Henry Tate	Chorley	Sugar magnate/gallery founder born in town
Sir Nigel Gresley	Swadlincote	Engineer lived near town
Sir Julian Huxley	Selsdon	UNESCO director-general supported local woodland project
Sir Walter Scott	Edinburgh	Airport pub in honour of local novelist/poet
Stanley Jefferson	Bishop Auckland	Jefferson (Stan Laurel) attended local school
Sweyn Forkbeard	Gainsborough	Danish king murdered in town
Thomas Telford	Ellesmere Port	Engineer worked on local infrastructure
Wilfred Owen	Oswestry	War poet baptized in town
William Morris	Hammersmith	Designer and craftsman lived nearby
William Morris	Oxford	Auto pioneer opened city's car factory
William Rufus	Carlisle	King who restored town to the English kingdom
William Webb Ellis	Twickenham	Inventor of rugby honoured near England HQ
William White	Nuneaton	White (comedian Larry Grayson) lived and died in town
William Wilberforce	Hull	Emancipation advocate was local MP
Woodrow Wilson	Carlisle	US President's mother born in town

CAMRA's Biggest Beer Festivals

	Festival	Attendance
1	Great British Beer Festival	67,000
2	Peterborough	43,000
3	Cambridge	34,500
4	Norwich	19,000
5	Nottingham	18,000
6	Great Welsh Beer & Cider Festival	17,300
7	Chelmsford	15,000
8	Reading	14,400
9	Worcester	12,000
10	Derby	10,000

Rules for Storing Bottled Beer

1 Always buy fresh stock

Some bottle-conditioned beers mature wonderfully in the bottle but most beer is undoubtedly best drunk young, so buy beers with plenty of time left before the 'best before' date.

2 Keep beers in a dark place

Light is an enemy of beer. If a beer is exposed to bright lights (sunlight or artificial), a chemical reaction can take place that leads to unpleasant flavours and 'skunky' aromas. For this reason, also be wary of beers packaged in clear or green bottles that are far less efficient than brown bottles in protecting beer from light.

3 Keep beers cool

As with all foodstuffs, low (but not freezing) temperatures help preserve beer. When it comes to serving the beer, check the temperature advice on the label.

4 Keep beers upright

This is not important with filtered beers but any beer that contains a sediment should be kept upright, or at least returned to the vertical well in advance of serving, to ensure the sediment remains at the bottom. For beers designed to be poured cloudy, this is not such an issue. Also beers with corked bottles need to be stored horizontally (to keep the cork moist and tight), but then returned to the upright well before serving.

Some Celebrities Who Have Advertised Beer

Celebrity	Beer
Jennifer Aniston	Heineken
Gina Bellman	Boddingtons
Victor Borge	Heineken
Susan Boyle	Yebisu
Anna Chancellor	Boddingtons
Chas and Dave	Courage Best
James Coburn	Schlitz Light
Billy Connolly	Kaliber
Peter Cook and Dudley Moore	Guinness
Lawrence Dallaglio	Greene King IPA
Paul Daniels and Debbie McGee	Heineken
Jack Dee	John Smith's
Douglas Fairbanks, Jnr and Gertrude Lawrence	Whitbread Pale Ale
Bryan Ferry	Carlsberg
Andrew Flintoff	Thwaites Lancaster Bomber
Harrison Ford	Kirin
Nick Hancock	Randalls
Rutger Hauer	Guinness
Paris Hilton	Devassa
Paul Hogan	Foster's
Englebert Humperdinck	John Smith's
Griff Rhys Jones	Holsten Pils
Peter Kay	John Smith's
Mr Magoo	Stag
James May	Fuller's London Pride
Rik Mayall	Wells Bombardier
Bernard Miles	Mackeson
Sarah Parish	Boddingtons
Brad Pitt	Heineken
Jonathan Ross	Harp
Melanie Sykes	Boddingtons
Holly Valance	Foster's Gold
Jean-Claude Van Damme	Coors Light
Orson Welles	Carlsberg
Ray Winstone	Holsten

Five Facts About Brewing Water

Water for brewing is only ever known as 'liquor' in a brewery. 'Water' is the stuff they use to hose down the floors and clean the vessels.

The mineral content of liquor is extremely important. To make a pilsner you need to use soft water; for a pale ale hard water is required.

Brewers are now able to strip out all minerals in water and replace them with the required minerals for the type of beer they wish to make.

For certain beer styles, useful minerals in water are calcium sulphate (encourages extract from both malt and hops, aids fermentation, reduces haze and increases acidity), magnesium sulphate (stimulates yeast) and calcium chloride (enhances sweetness and body).

Re-creating the distinct gypsum- and magnesium-rich waters that made the town of Burton-on-Trent so important for pale ale production is known as burtonization.

The Bad Beer Guide

A poor pint of beer is something, unfortunately, we all encounter at some point. But what, exactly, could be wrong with the beer? To help, here's a simple checklist of common faults found in badly-kept real ale.

Appearance	Likely Cause
Warm to the taste	Slow turnover; warm beer lines
Warm to the touch	Newly-washed glass
Flat and insipid – lacks character	Old cask
Hazy (but fresh taste – often apples or sulphur)	Fresh cask still to settle
Cloudy (often with undesirable tastes)	Yeast/bacteria in suspension; old cask
Unusual/undesirable tastes (sour, parsnip, celery, sweat)	Bacterial infection
Other unusual/undesirable tastes (TCP, sewers, wood, plastic, creosote)	Wild yeast infection

Study at the Academy

Founded in 2003, The Beer Academy is an educational body dedicated to spreading the word about beer and its safe enjoyment. Through courses, seminars and tastings, it helps inspire both those working in the industry in the UK and those whom the industry serves, with the emphasis on taste training, beer and food pairing, and other issues.

Types of Malts

It is not possible to brew with raw barley. Barley has to be treated in order to release starches that can be converted by natural enzymes in the grain during the brewing process into sugars for fermentation. To achieve this, the barley is malted. This involves soaking and partially germinating the grain and then halting germination by heating it in a kiln. The amount of heat applied and the length of time in the kiln also affect the character of the malt, in both its colour and its taste. The table below shows the most common types of malt produced for brewing. Their colours are defined according to two scales. One is stipulated by a technical body called the European Brewing Convention; the other is known as degrees Lovibond, after the brewer who devised the scale in the 19th century. Both scales give the lightest colours the lowest figures.

Malt Type	Approx. ECB/ Lovibond Colour	Common Uses
Lager or pilsner malt	2.5/1.5	Lagers, blonde/summer ales
Pale malt	4.5/2.2	Ales
Vienna malt	5–8/2.4–2.8	Amber lagers, Märzen
Mild ale malt	9–15/3.9–6.2	Milds
Munich malt	12–15/5.1–6.2	Dark lagers
Amber malt	65/25	Victorian-style ales
Crystal malt	145/55	Amber ales
Brown malt	110/42	Porters
Chocolate malt	1060/400	Dark milds, stouts, porters
Black malt	1280/480	Stouts, porters
Wheat malt	3/1.7	Wheat beers, ales
Roasted barley	1220/460	Stouts, porters

Information supplied by Warminster Maltings Ltd.

Great American Beer Festival Categories

The USA's premier beer competition judges in the following categories.

Lager Beer Styles

American-Style or
  International-Style Pilsener
German-Style Pilsener
Bohemian-Style Pilsener
Munich-Style Helles
Dortmunder or
  German-Style Oktoberfest
American-Style Lager, Light Lager
  or Premium Lager
American-Style Specialty Lager
  or Cream Ale or Lager

Vienna-Style Lager
German-Style Märzen
American-Style Amber Lager
European-Style Dunkel
American-Style Dark Lager
German-Style Schwarzbier
Bock
German-Style Doppelbock
  or Eisbock
Baltic-Style Porter

Ale Beer Styles

Golden or Blonde Ale
German-Style Kölsch
English-Style Summer Ale
Classic English-Style Pale Ale
English-Style India Pale Ale
International-Style Pale Ale
American-Style Pale Ale
American-Style Strong Pale Ale
American-Style India Pale Ale
Imperial India Pale Ale
American-Style Amber/Red Ale
Imperial Red Ale
English-Style Mild Ale
Ordinary or Special Bitter
Extra Special Bitter
Scottish-Style Ale
Irish-Style Red Ale
English-Style Brown Ale
American-Style Brown Ale
American-Style Black Ale
German-Style Altbier

German-Style Sour Ale
South German-Style Hefeweizen
German-Style Wheat Ale
Belgian-Style Witbier
French- and Belgian-Style Saison
Belgian- and French-Style Ale
Belgian-Style Lambic or Sour Ale
Belgian-Style Abbey Ale
Belgian-Style Strong Specialty Ale
Brown Porter
Robust Porter
Classic Irish-Style Dry Stout
Foreign-Style Stout
American-Style Stout
Sweet Stout
Oatmeal Stout
Imperial Stout
Scotch Ale
Old Ale or Strong Ale
Barley Wine-Style Ale

Hybrid/Mixed Styles

American-Style Wheat Beer

American-Style Wheat Beer
  With Yeast

Fruit Beer

Fruit Wheat Beer

Field Beer or Pumpkin Beer

Herb and Spice Beer

Chocolate Beer

Coffee Beer

Specialty Beer

Rye Beer

Specialty Honey Beer

Session Beer

Other Strong Beer

Experimental Beer

Indigenous Beer

Gluten-Free Beer

American-Belgo-Style Ale

American-Style Sour Ale

American-Style Brett Ale

Wood- and Barrel-Aged Beer

Wood- and Barrel-Aged Strong
  Beer

Wood- and Barrel-Aged Strong
  Stout

Wood- and Barrel-Aged Sour Beer

Aged Beer

Kellerbier or Zwickelbier

Smoke Beer

Categories used in 2011. Additionally, many of the above categories are broken down into sub-categories.

Champion Beer of Britain Categories

Champion Beer of Britain is the UK's premier competition for cask- and bottle-conditioned beers. The contest, based on ten, broadly-based categories, is judged each August during the Great British Beer Festival.

Bitter	Speciality Beer
Best Bitter	Bottle-conditioned Beer
Strong Bitter/Ale	Old Ale/Strong Mild*
Golden Ale	Barley Wine*
Mild	Stout & Porter*

*Judged at the Champion Winter Beer of Britain contest, during CAMRA's National Festival of Winter Ales in January.

Double Champion

The only beer to win CAMRA's Champion Beer of Britain contest two years in a row is Brewers Gold from Crouch Vale in Essex, in 2005–6.

UK Excise Duty Rates Since 1950

Excise duty is the tax paid by brewers on the beers they produce, a charge which is passed on to customers as part of the price of a pint. The following figures show the UK excise duty, in pence, that has been levied over the years per pint for a beer with an original gravity of 1037*

1950	3.29	1980	8.60
1959	2.58	1981	11.86
1961	2.84	1982	13.44
1964	3.23	1983	14.23
1965	3.62	1984	15.81
1966	3.99	1985	17.00
1968	4.39	1988	17.79
1973	2.91	1990	19.17
1974	3.77	1991	20.95
1975	5.51	1992	21.90
1976	6.38	1993	22.99
1977	7.01		

Excise duty, in pence, levied per pint for a beer of 4.0% ABV**

1993	23.75	2006	30.14
1995	24.59	2007	31.16
1998	25.32	2008 (March)	34.00
1999	26.14	2008 (December)	36.71
2000	27.03	2009	37.44
2003	27.78	2010	39.37
2004	28.61	2011	42.20
2005	29.37		

Years shown are those when changes in duty rate took place.

*Until 31 May 1993, duty on beer was levied according to the original gravity of the wort prior to pitching the yeast for fermentation. A wastage allowance of 6% was given, as not all the wort would have gone on to be finished beer.

**Since 1 June 1993, excise duty has been based on the alcoholic strength of the finished beer.

Note: In 2002, Progressive Beer Duty was introduced for brewers producing fewer than 30,000 hectolitres a year. In 2004, Progressive Beer Duty was extended to brewers producing up to 60,000 hectolitres a year.

Stately Home Breweries

Country house brewing is largely a thing of the past but there are still some stately homes in Britain where brewing takes place, if not in the hall or associated buildings themselves then within the estate's lands.

Brewery	Location	Stately Home
Elveden*	Thetford, Norfolk	Elveden Hall
North Yorkshire	Guisborough, North Yorkshire	Pinchinthorpe Hall
Peak Ales	Chatsworth, Derbyshire	Chatsworth
Prior's Well	Hardwick, Nottinghamshire	Clumber Park
Shugborough**	Stafford	Shugborough Hall
St Peter's	St Peter South Elmham, Suffolk	St Peter's Hall
Thornbridge***	Ashford-in-the-Water, Derbyshire	Thornbridge Hall
Traquair	Innerleithen, Borders	Traquair House
Welbeck Abbey	Worksop, Nottinghamshire	Welbeck Abbey
Wentworth	Rotherham, South Yorkshire	Wentworth Woodhouse

*Operated by Iceni Brewery. ** Operated by Titanic Brewery.

***Also has new larger brewery off site.

Whatever Happened to Watney's?

In the 1960s and '70s, London-based Watney's was one of the leading purveyors of pressurized keg bitter – bland, pasteurized, artificially carbonated beer that was threatening to kill off traditional, cask-conditioned ale. Watney's Red Barrel was the product that led the way, morphing into Watney's Red in the 1970s. The brewery became an object of both derision and distaste for CAMRA pioneers. Bill Tidy in his *Keg Buster* cartoon strip dubbed the company 'Grotney's', and the first ever *Good Beer Guide* needed to be pulped and hastily re-edited on legal advice to change a comment about Watney's beer from 'avoid like the plague' to 'avoid at all costs'. Thankfully, Watney's Red didn't last and the company was taken over by the hospitality group Grand Metropolitan, which in turn merged its brewing interests with Courage in the 1990s.

Ten Beers to Try Before You Die!

Roger Protz, long-serving editor of the *Good Beer Guide* and author of the best-selling *300 Beers to Try Before You Die!*, among numerous beer books, narrows his excellent selection to just ten must-drink beers. His chosen beers – the distillation of more than 35 years of professional beer tasting experience – are arranged here solely in alphabetical order.

I   Burton Bridge Empire Pale Ale
Brewed – of course – in Burton-on-Trent, this bottle-conditioned beer is matured in the brewery for six months to replicate the long sea journey to India endured by Victorian IPAs. Biscuity malt, spicy hops, orange fruit – superb.

2   Jever Pilsener
A pils with a hairy chest: Frieslanders demand bitter beers and Jever lives up to the challenge with a herbal, grassy and resinous hop character, toasted malt and a hint of honey sweetness to balance the intense bitterness.

3   Holt's Mild
A Manchester phenomenon, only 3.2% ABV but bursting with Golding and Northdown hops that create 30 units of bitterness – high for a mild. The bitterness is balanced by chocolate, liquorice and tart, burnt fruit notes. Remarkable.

4   Coopers Sparkling Ale
The Cooper family in Adelaide kept the ale flag flying through the dog days of Foster's and XXXX. It now leads the craft beer renaissance Down Under with a beer with a peppery note from Pride of Ringwood hops, the bitterness balanced by juicy malt and tart citrus fruit. The perfect way to say 'G'day'.

5   Harveys Sussex Best Bitter
A classic and under-rated traditional copper-coloured bitter with no fewer than four English hops bringing a pungent, grassy and spicy note to the beer. English malts add a lush grain character, and malt and hops are overlaid by tangy citrus fruit. A delight.

6 Timothy Taylor Landlord

An uncompromising Yorkshire best bitter brewed with pure spring water, Golden Promise malt (more of a whisky malt than a beer one) and Fuggle and Golding hops. The stunning lemon fruit note that permeates the beer is the result of the hopped wort circulating over a bed of Styrian Goldings prior to fermentation.

7 Anker Gouden Carolus Classic

It lives up to the classic claim: brewed in Mechelen in Belgium, the beer celebrates a gold coin minted to honour the reign of the Habsburg emperor Charles V, who grew up in the town. Five malts and Golding hops combine to produce aromas and flavours of port wine, chocolate, spices and raisins.

8 Sierra Nevada Bigfoot Barleywine Style Ale

You expect barley wines of 9.6% ABV to present lots of rich malt and fruit but Bigfoot uses three hops from Washington State – Cascade, Centennial and Chinook – to impart a complex bitter, piny and citrus note to the beer, balancing the rich grain and the warming alcohol character. Because of the beer's strength, it will improve with ageing.

9 Meantime London Porter

Porter's roots are in London, and Meantime Brewing in the south-east part of the capital city has created a fine interpretation of the style. At 6.5% ABV it's a highly complex beer, brewed with seven malts and Fuggle and Golding hops. The finished beer offers chocolate, espresso, vanilla, smoked malt and liquorice, backed by peppery and bitter hops.

10 Westmalle Tripel

And finally … arguably the best beer in the world. Created by Belgian Trappist monks in a beautiful Art Deco brewhouse, Tripel at 9.5% ABV is orange/gold, brewed with pilsner malt and hopped with Tettnang, Saaz and Styrian varieties. Saaz-inspired, floral hop aroma with orange fruit, a tangy, fruity, hoppy palate and a long finish full of sappy malt, hop resins and a herbal note. One word sums it all up: heavenly.

The Definition of Real Ale

'Real ale, a name sometimes applied to draught beer
that has been brewed and stored in the traditional way,
and which has undergone secondary fermentation of the yeast
in the container from which it is dispensed;
also called "cask-conditioned" beer.'

Oxford English Dictionary, 2nd Edition (1989)

'Beer' and 'Brewery' in Other Languages

Language	Beer	Brewery
Bulgarian	bira	pivovarna
Chinese	pi jiu	niang jiu chang
Croatian	pivo	pivovara
Czech	pivo	pivovar
Danish	øl	bryggeri
Dutch	bier	brouwerij
Esperanto	biero	bierfarejo
Estonian	õlu	õllevabrik
Finnish	olut	olutpanimo
French	bière	brasserie
Gaelic	beoir	grúdlann
German	bier	brauerei
Greek	bira	zythopoieío
Hungarian	sör	sörfozde
Italian	birra	birreria
Japanese	biiru	jouzousho
Latvian	alus	alus daritava
Norwegian	øl	bryggeri
Polish	piwo	browar
Portuguese	cerveja	cervejaria
Romanian	bere	berar
Russian	pivo	pivovarennyjzavod
Spanish	cerveza	cervecería
Swedish	öl	bryggeri
Welsh	cwrw	bragdy

Who Was Samuel Adams?

Samuel Adams lends his name to a huge selection of beers in various styles produced by the Boston Beer Company. His image also appears on bottle labels, suggesting that the man who has helped drive forward the American craft brewing revolution of the 20th and 21st centuries was actually a key figure in another kind of revolution 200 years earlier. In fact, Adams was born 1722, into a Boston brewing family, but politics became his profession, with opposition to British rule his driving force. He was later a signatory on the American Declaration of Independence.

The World's Biggest Beer Brands

	Brand	Million US Barrels
1	Budweiser	75.4
2	Snow (China)	61.7
3	Skol	31.2
4	Miller	28.1
5	Corona	27.7
6	Brahma	25.3
7	Tsingtao	25.2
8	Heineken	24.3
9	Coors	22.3
10	Asahi	19.1

Figures given are for 2009. Brands include brand extensions such as light beers.

Source: Impact Databank.

The Beer Mat House

Ever wondered what to do with 300,000 beer mats? Well, German Sven Goebel was not stuck for inspiration. In 2010, he decided to build a 'house of cards'-style structure – a sort of five-room apartment, complete with furniture – to gain a place in the *Guinness Book of World Records*. The painstaking construction took more than three months and then Goebel had to knock it all down to prove it was not held together with anything other than the weight of the cards themselves and static electricity. And the beer advertised on the mats? It was Gaffel Kölsch.

How Strong Do We Like It?

Below is the average strength of beer as sold in a selection of countries.

Country	ABV	Country	ABV
France	6.0%	Germany	4.8%
Spain	5.7%	Hungary	4.8%
Belgium & Luxembourg	5.2%	Romania	4.8%
Portugal	5.1%	Russian Federation	4.8%
Canada	5.0%	Switzerland	4.8%
Japan	5.0%	Denmark	4.6%
Lithuania	5.0%	Finland	4.6%
Netherlands	5.0%	USA	4.6%
Poland	5.0%	Czech Republic	4.5%
South Africa	5.0%	Slovak Republic	4.5%
Austria	4.9%	Sweden	4.5%
Greece	4.9%	Ireland	4.3%
Italy	4.9%	Norway	4.3%
Australia	4.8%	United Kingdom	4.2%
Bulgaria	4.8%	New Zealand	4.0%

Figures given are for 2008. Source: British Beer & Pub Association Statistical Handbook 2010.

Beer Heroes: George Bateman (1927–2007)

In the mid 1980s, Lincolnshire regional brewer Batemans faced a crisis. The board of the family-owned company was split, with two directors wanting to sell the business and chairman George Bateman desperate to keep Batemans brewing. He faced an uphill task. His brother and sister, who planned to sell, controlled 60 per cent of the shares, so George – a passionate advocate of the independent brewing sector – embarked on a marathon effort to raise funds to buy them out. If he failed, Batemans' brewing days were numbered. Spurred on by the support of real ale campaigners, his late wife Pat, and children Stuart and Jaclyn, who now run the business, George eventually succeeded in acquiring the funds to keep the Wainfleet brewhouse open. Batemans remains one of Britain's most cherished breweries, its beers savoured by drinkers locally, nationally and internationally, but it so very nearly became just another evocative name in the register of lost producers.

Beers With Unusual Ingredients

Beer	Brewery	Ingredient(s)
Alba	Williams Bros	Pine sprigs
Banana Bread Beer	Charles Wells	Bananas
Blandford Fly	Hall & Woodhouse	Ginger
Bracia	Thornbridge	Chestnut honey
Chalky's Bite	Sharp's	Fennel seeds
Chipotle Ale	Rogue Ales	Chipotle peppers
Cranberry Wheat	Iceni	Cranberries
Desperados	Fischer	Tequila
Double Chocolate Stout	Young's	Chocolate
Ebulum	Williams Bros	Elderberry
Fine Raisin Beer	Cains	Californian raisins
Fraoch	Williams Bros	Heather flowers
Gageleer	Proef	Sweet gale
Golden Champion	Hall & Woodhouse	Elderflowers
Golden Glory	Hall & Woodhouse	Peach blossom
Grozet	Williams Bros	Gooseberries
Hanfblüte	Appenzeller	Hemp
Hazelnut Brown Nectar	Rogue Ales	Hazelnuts
Jack Frost	Fuller's	Blackberries
Joseph	Silenrieux	Spelt
Kelpie	Williams Bros	Seaweed
Maple Moon	Holt	Maple
Morimoto Soba Ale	Rogue Ales	Soba (buckwheat)
O-Rosie	Otley	Rosemary
Original Port Stout	O'Hanlon's	Port
Original Porter	Shepherd Neame	Liquorice
Oyster Stout	Porterhouse	Oysters
Pietra	Pietra	Chestnut flour
Red, White & Blueberry	Iceni	Blueberries
Róisin	Williams Bros	Tayberries
Stinger	Hall & Woodhouse	Nettles
Swordfish	Wadworth	Rum
Thai Bo	Otley	Lemongrass, galangal, lime leaf
Umbel Ale	Nethergate	Coriander
Waggle Dance	Young's	Honey

Extreme British Breweries

Northernmost: Valhalla Brewery, Unst, Shetland Islands
Easternmost: Green Jack, Lowestoft, Suffolk
Southernmost: Ales of Scilly, St Mary, Isles of Scilly
Westernmost: Hebridean Brewing Company, Stornoway, Isle of Lewis

Want to Learn How to Brew?

Several international establishments offer educational and training courses in brewing. Below are the most prominent (varying degrees of brewing competence are addressed: courses are not just for beginners).

Country	Establishment
Australia	University of Ballarat, Victoria www.ballarat.edu.au
Denmark	Scandinavian School of Brewing, Valby, Copenhagen www.brewingschool.dk
Germany	Doemans Academy, Munich www.doemans.org VLB, Berlin www.vlb-berlin.org Weihenstephan Technical University, Munich www.wzw.tum.de
UK	Brewlab, University of Sunderland www.brewlab.co.uk International Centre for Brewing & Distilling, Heriot-Watt University, Edinburgh www.icbd.hw.ac.uk Institute of Brewing & Distilling, London www.ibd.org.uk University of Nottingham pgstudy.nottingham.ac.uk
USA	American Brewers Guild, Salisbury, Vermont www.abgbrew.com Master Brewers Association of the Americas, St Paul, Minnesota www.mbaa.com Siebel Institute of Technology, Chicago, Illinois www.siebelinstitute.com University of California – Davis, California www.universityextension.ucdavis.edu/brewing

Gone to the Dogs

In Australia, there's a beer specifically brewed for dogs. DB Dog Beer is designed to satisfy canine thirsts for beer, without causing any health problems. The beer is alcohol free, non carbonated and tastes of beef.

The World's Biggest Brewing Companies

	Company	Million US Barrels
1	Anheuser-Busch InBev	305.7
2	SABMiller	181.2
3	Heineken	141.2
4	Carlsberg	98.9
5	China Resources Enterprise	71.3
6	Tsingtao	50.9
7	Grupo Modelo	44.8
8	Molson Coors	42.6
9	Beijing Yanjing Beer Group	39.8
10	Kirin	27.8

Figures given are for 2009. Source: Impact Databank.

Skunky Beer

Beer bottles generally come in three colours, brown, green and clear. Brown bottles may be less sexy than green and clear glass but they do a far better job in protecting the contents from light. Both sunlight and artificial light can cause problems for beer. The light reacts with chemicals in the hops to create compounds that, although unharmful, change the flavour profile of the beer. In particular, the aroma of the beer can become rather vegetal or rubbery and this is very obvious on opening the bottle. In America, they call the unpleasant smell 'skunky' but, as the skunk doesn't live in most parts of the world, the analogy is not always recognized by non-Americans. Green bottles are marginally better than clear glass, which is ineffective, but for beer flavour protection brown remains by far the best option. Some breweries, determined to sell their beer in clear glass, even go as far as using modified hop extracts to prevent the light reaction from taking place.

CAMRA's Champion Bottled Beers

This contest is judged as part of CAMRA's Champion Beer of Britain competition every August and is dedicated to bottle-conditioned beers.

1991	Worthington's White Shield (Bass)*
1992	Gale's Prize Old Ale
1993	Eldridge Pope Thomas Hardy's Ale
1994	Courage Imperial Russian Stout**
1995	King & Barnes Festive**
1996	Marston's Oyster Stout***
1997	Hop Back Summer Lightning
1998	Fuller's 1845
1999	Young's Special London Ale
2000	Worthington's White Shield (King & Barnes)*
2001	RCH Ale Mary
2002	Fuller's 1845
2003	O'Hanlon's Original Port Stout
2004	Titanic Stout
2005	Durham Evensong
2006	Worthington's White Shield (Coors)*
2007	O'Hanlon's Original Port Stout
2008	Wye Valley Dorothy Goodbody's Wholesome Stout
2009	Titanic Stout
2010	St Austell Admiral's Ale
2011	St Austell Proper Job

*Beer changed brewery. **No longer in production.

***No longer bottle-conditioned.

The National Brewery Centre

Housed in premises formerly occupied by the Bass Museum and the Coors Visitor Centre in Burton-on-Trent, The National Brewery Centre is a showcase for Britain's great brewing culture, providing a lively insight into how beer is produced and how times have changed. A collection of vintage brewery vehicles, shire horses, a scale model of Burton as it was in 1921 and the working William Worthington's microbrewery are just some of the many family-oriented attractions the centre now offers.

Breweries and Tents Featured at Oktoberfest

The world-famous Oktoberfest – an enormous, raucous celebration of Bavarian beer – is staged in Munich in mid-September (despite its name) every year. The event commemorates the marriage, in 1810, of the future King Ludwig I of Bavaria and Princess Therese of Saxony. Only six breweries are allowed to partake and run the impressive beer tents (akin to giant halls), all of them having bases within the city of Munich (although four of the six are now owned by multi-national companies).

Tent (translation, if appropriate)	Brewery
1 Hippodrom (Hippodrome)	Spaten-Franziskaner (A-B InBev)
2 Armbrustschützenzelt (Crossbow Tent)	Paulaner (Heineken)
3 Hofbräuzelt (Hofbräu Tent)	Hofbräu
4 Hacker-Festzelt (Hacker Tent)	Hacker-Pschorr (Heineken)
5 Schottenhamel	Spaten-Franziskaner (A-B InBev)
6 Winzerer Fähndl	Paulaner (Heineken)
7 Schützen-Festzelt	Löwenbräu (A-B InBev)
8 Käfer's Wies'n-Schänke	Paulaner (Heineken)
9 Weinzelt (Wine Tent)	Paulaner (Heineken)
10 Löwenbräu-Festhall (Löwenbräu Tent)	Löwenbräu (A-B InBev)
11 Bräurosl	Hacker-Pschorr (Heineken)
12 Augustiner-Festhalle (Augustiner Tent)	Augustiner
13 Ochsenbraterei (Ox Grill)	Spaten-Franziskaner (A-B InBev)
14 Fischer-Vroni (Fish Grill)	Augustiner

Don't Spit, Swallow!

Unlike wine judges, professional beer tasters do not spit out their beer. This is because certain flavours become more apparent after you've swallowed. Sweetness and maltiness tend to subside, but hop character, bitterness and dryness are often accentuated. Brewers have considered all of this when creating beers, so don't let them down. Enjoy the finish!

Important Brewing Museums

Austria
Salzburg   *Stiegl's Brauwelt*, Bräuhausstrasse 9.
                  Tel. + 43 662 8387-1492 www.brauwelt.at
                  The fun of beer production at a working brewery.

Belgium
Alveringem   *Mout- en Brouwhuis De Snoek*, Fortem 40.
                  Tel + 32 58 28 96 74 www.desnoek.be
                  Pre-industrial age brewing exhibited.

Bocholt   *Bocholter Brouwerijmuseum*, Dorpsstraat 53.
                  Tel. + 32 89 48 16 76
                  www.bocholterbrouwerijmuseum.be
                  Said to be the largest brewery museum in Europe.

Brussels   *Brussels Gueuze Museum*, Gheudestraat 56.
                  Tel. + 32 2 521 49 28 www.cantillon.be
                  A working lambic beer museum.

Poperinge   *National Hop Museum*, Gasthuisstraat 71.
                  Tel. +32 57 33 79 22 www.hopmuseum.be
                  The skills of hop cultivation divulged.

Czech Republic
Pilsen   *The Brewery Museum*, Veleslavinova 6.
                  Tel. +420 377 235574 www.prazdroj.cz
                  A homage to pilsner in the very place it was created.

Zatec   *Chmelařské Hop Museum*, náměstí Prokopa Velkého.
                  Tel. + 420 415 710315 www.muzeum@chmelarstvi.cz
                  The history of hop cultivation in the Saaz region.

France
Stenay   *Musée Européen de la Bière*, Rue du Moulin 17.
                  Tel. +33 3 29 80 68 78 www.musee-de-la-biere.com
                  Large, well-established museum in a former maltings.

Germany
Bamberg   *Fränkisches Brauereimuseum*, Michelsberg 10f.
                  www.brauereimuseum.org
                  The brewing heritage of this outstanding beer region.

Kulmbach	*Bavarian Brewery Museum*, Hofer Strasse 20.
	Tel. + 49 9221 805 14
	www.bayerisches-brauereimuseum.de
	Explore the roots of Bavarian brewing.

Ireland
Dublin	*Guinness Storehouse*, St James's Gate.
	Tel. + 353 1 408 4800 www.guinness-storehouse.com
	The story of the black stuff.

Japan
Sapporo	*Sapporo Beer Museum*
	Tel. + 81 11 731 4368 www.sapporobeer.jp/english
	Free museum attracting 1.5 million visitors a year.

Netherlands
Alkmaar	*Nationaal Biermuseum 'De Boom'*, Houttil 1.
	Tel. + 31 72 511 3801 www.biermuseum.nl
	The Netherlands' original brewing museum.

Amsterdam	*Heineken Experience*, Stadhouderskade 78.
	Tel. + 31 20 523 9435 www.heinekenexperience.com
	Museum in the old brewery with various attractions,
	including the chance to ride on a bottling line.

UK
Burton-upon-Trent	*National Brewery Centre*, Horninglow Street.
	Tel. 01283 532880 www.nationalbrewerycentre.co.uk
	Formerly the Bass Museum/Coors Visitor Centre:
	a fascinating insight into Burton's brewing heritage.

Bury St Edmunds	*Greene King Visitor Centre*, Westgate Street
	Tel. 01284 714297 www.greeneking.co.uk
	Trappings of the company's history displayed.

Newton Abbot	*Tucker's Maltings*, Teign Road.
	Tel. 01626 334734 www.edwintucker.com
	See a traditional floor maltings at work.

USA
Pennsylvania	*Yuengling Brewery*,
	5th & Mahantongo Streets, Pottsville.
	Tel. + 1 570 628 4890 www.yuengling.com
	Behind the scenes of one of America's oldest breweries.

Royal Wedding Beers

Listed below are some of the many beers created by British brewers to celebrate the wedding of Prince William and Kate Middleton in 2011.

Beer	Brewery
Better Half	Wadworth
Consummation Ale	Truman's
Gotcha Will!	Leek
Hoppy NuptiAle	Verulam
HRH (His Royal Honeymoon)	Blackfriars
I Will	Chiltern; Teignworthy; Wold Top
Kate Loves Willy	Skinner's
Kiss Me Kate	Castle Rock; Jennings; Kinver
Matrimoniale	Westerham
Middleton to Windsor	Shepherd Neame
Middleton's	Lees
Nuptial Nectar	Wincle
Perfect Union	Marston's
Prince of Ales	Wells & Young's
Republic Revolution	Brodie's
Royal Appointment	Moorhouse's
Royal Box	Box Steam
Royal Flush	Enville; Wolf
Royal Kiss	Southport
Royal Match	Moodley's
Royal Nuptial Ale	Harveys
Royal Splice	Banks's
Royal Union	Vale
Royal Virility Performance	BrewDog
Royally Brewtiful	Peak
Seal of Approval	Ulverston
Something Blue	Durham
White Wedding	Welton's
Will I Do	Ramsbury
William Wins-Her	Quartz
Willy's Crown Jewels	Batemans
Windsor Knot	Elgood's; Goddards; Windsor & Eton
WnK Royal Ale	Blue Anchor

Community-Owned British Pubs

Some pubs that have been collectively purchased by their customers.

The Angel Inn, Grosmont, Gwent
The Beauchamp Arms, Dymock, Gloucestershire*
The Cherry Tree Inn, Cherry Willingham, Lincolnshire
The Crown, Clunton, Shropshire
The Farriers Arms, Mersham, Kent
The George & Dragon, Hudswell, North Yorkshire
The Grey Bull, Stanhope, County Durham
The Greyhound, Grizebeck, Cumbria**
The Jolly Farmer, Cookham Dean, Berkshire
The New Inn, Shipton Gorge, Dorset**
The Norton, Cold Norton, Essex
The Old Crown, Hesket Newmarket, Cumbria
The Old Thirteenth Cheshire Astley Volunteer Rifleman Corps Inn,
  Stalybridge, Greater Manchester
The Plough, Horbling, Lincolnshire*
The Raven Inn, Llanarmon-y-Lal, Denbighshire**
The Red Lion, Preston, Hertfordshire
The Royal Oak Inn, Meavy, Devon*
The Sherlock Inn, Sherlock Row, Berkshire
The Star Inn, Salford, Greater Manchester
Tafarn y fic, Llithfaen, Gwynedd
The Three Horseshoes, Thursley, Surrey
The Tiger Inn, Stowting, Kent

*Owned by the parish council.

**Leased by the community.

Beer Cocktails Are Banned

In the US state of Nebraska it is illegal to serve beer cocktails. That means any combination of beer and a spirit in a glass is not allowed. Other types of cocktails are permitted, however, and combining various spirits in a glass is totally above board. It is believed the bizarre law dates back to the dark days of Prohibition when dodgers of the alcohol ban in force at the time took to injecting spirits into non-alcoholic beer.

The Noble Hops

Four strains of continental hops have been revered for centuries for their elegant bitterness and aromas. They are known as the Noble Hops.

Hallertauer Mittelfrüh   Spalt   Tettnanger   Saaz

Beers Named After Famous Vehicles

Beer	Brewery	Country
Ark Royal (ship)	Wapping	UK
Bluebird (land and water speed craft)	Coniston	UK
Concorde (aircraft)	Cottage	UK
Dreadnought (ship)	Chalk Hill	UK
	Nottingham	UK
Elissa IPA (ship)	Saint Arnold	USA
Endeavour (ship)	Cropton	UK
Endurance (ship)	Cambrinus	UK
Golden Arrow (steam engine)	Cottage	UK
Golden Hinde (ship)	Coastal	UK
Herald (aircraft)	Cottage	UK
HMS Bounty Old Ale (ship)	Dry Dock	USA
HMS Victory ESB (ship)	Dry Dock	USA
HMS Warrior (ship)	Itchen Valley	UK
Hurricane (aircraft)	Crouch Vale	UK
Invincible (ship)	Irving	UK
Lancaster Bomber (aircraft)	Thwaites	UK
Mallard IPA (steam engine)	Cottage	UK
Mary Rose (ship)	East Coast	UK
Mayflower (ship)	Mayflower	USA
Old Speckled Hen (an MG car)	Greene King	UK
Puffing Billy (steam engine)	Cottage	UK
Rocket (steam engine)	Wylam	UK
Spitfire (aircraft)	Shepherd Neame	UK
SS Great Britain (ship)	Cottage	UK
Sunbeam Tiger (car)	Cottage	UK
USS Enterprise IPA (space ship)	Dry Dock	USA
Vanguard (ship)	Irving	UK

The Power of Marketing

'The big brewers have been so successful in their promotion of pressurised
beers that millions of people are growing up without ever having the chance
to taste real ale. And when they do get the chance, they are likely to
choose pressurised beer instead – because that's what the television adverts
tell them to drink. They become so accustomed to the taste of pressurised
beer that they will not – or cannot – drink the real thing.'

From the first edition of the *Good Beer Guide*, published 1974.

British Beer Imports

	Country	'000 barrels
1	Ireland	1,783.7
2	Germany	817.9
3	Netherlands	640.7
4	Italy	492.7
5	Mexico	393.8
6	France	340.0
7	Belgium & Luxembourg	168.5
8	Spain	139.4
9	Czech Republic	126.6
10	Poland	70.4
11	Singapore	42.0
12	Portugal	32.1
13	USA	21.4
14	China	21.1
15	Thailand	15.6
	Other countries	93.4

Figures given are for 2009. Source: British Beer & Pub Association Statistical Handbook 2010.

Strange Tribute

Kenya's leading beer export, Tusker Lager, was actually named after an
elephant that killed the founder of the brewery. The beer was already in
production before George Hurst met his unfortunate demise, during
a hunting expedition in 1923, but was then renamed in his memory.

The Brewers of Europe

The Brewers of Europe is a European-wide trade association with 24 members (from the EU) and three associate members. It was established in 1958 and works to promote and protect the interests of Europe's brewing industry. The association's headquarters can be found at: Rue Caroly 23–25, 1050 Brussels, Belgium; www.brewersofeurope.org.

Austria: *Verband der Brauereien Österreichs*   www.bierserver.at
   Zaunergasse 1–3, A-1030 Vienna
Belgium: *Belgian Brewers*   www.beerparadise.be
   Maison des Brasseurs, Grand'Place 10, B-1000 Brussels
Bulgaria: *UBB – Union of Brewers in Bulgaria*   www.pivovari.com
   16 Bacho Kiro Street, 1000 Sofia
Cyprus: *Cyprus Brewers Association*
   PO Box 21455, 1509 Nicosia
Czech Republic: *Czech Beer and Malt Association*   www.cspas.cz
   Lipova 15, CZ-120 44 Praha, 2
Denmark: *Bryggeriforeningen*   www.bryggeriforeningen.dk
   Faxehus, Gamle Carlsberg Vej 16, DK-2500 Valby
Finland: *Panimoliitto –*   www.panimoliitto.fi
   Finnish Federation of the Brewing Industry
   Pasilankatu 2, PO Box 115, FIN-00241 Helsinki
France: *Brasseurs de France*   www.brasseurs-de-france.com
   Bd Malesherbes 25, F-75008 Paris
Germany: *Deutscher Brauer-Bund e.V.*   www.brauer-bund.de
   Neustädische Kirchstrasse 7a, D-10117 Berlin
Greece: *Greek Brewers' Association*
   107 Kifissou Ave, GR-122 41 Egaleo
Hungary: *Association of Hungarian Brewers*   www.sorszovetseg.hu
   Fehérhajó utca 8–10, 111/1, 1052-Budapest
Ireland: *The Irish Brewers' Association*   www.abfi.ie
   Confederation House, 84–86 Lower Baggot Street, Dublin 2
Italy: *Associazione degli Industriali della Birra e del Malto*   www.assobirra.it
   Viale di Val Fiorita 90, I-00144 Rome
Lithuania: *Lithuanian Breweries Association*
   J Jasinskio 16b, LT-01112 Vilnius
Luxembourg: *Féderation des Brasseurs Luxembourgeois*
   Rue Alcide de Gaspéri, 7, BP 1304, L-1013 Luxembourg-Kirchberg

Malta: *The Malta Chamber of Commerce,*   www.maltachamber.org.mt
Enterprise and Industry
Exchange Buildings, Republic Street, Valetta VLT 1117
Netherlands: *Nederlandse Brouwers*   www.nederlandsebrouwers.nl
Dagelijkse Groenmarkt 3–5, NL-2513 Den Haag
Norway: *Norwegian Brewers**   www.bryggeriforeningen.no
Sorkedalsveien 6, PO Box 7087 Majorstuen, N-0306 Oslo
Poland: *The Union of Brewing Industry*   www.browary-polskie.pl
Employers in Poland
Biuro Zarzadu Zwiazku, Al. Jana Pawla II 12 lok. 739, 00-124 Warsaw
Portugal: *APCV – Associação Portuguesa dos*   www.apcv.pt
Produtores de Cerveja
Edificio Empresarial EE3, Pólo Tecnológico de Lisboa,
Lote 3, P-1600-546 Lisbon
Romania: *Brewers of Romania*   www.berariiromaniei.ro
10 Poterasi Street, 2nd Floor, Bucharest 4
Slovakia: *Slovak Beer and Malt Association*
Zahradnicka 21, 811 07 Bratislava
Spain: *Cerveceros de España*   www.cerveceros.org
Almagro 24 – 2° Izda., E-28010 Madrid
Sweden: *Sveriges Bryggerier* AB   www.sverigesbryggerier.se
Grev Turegatan, 9, 1tr, S-114 46 Stockholm
Switzerland: *Schweizer Brauerei-Verband**   www.bier.ch
Engimattstrasse 11, PO Box 2124, CH-8027 Zürich
Turkey: *Beer and Malt Producers' Association of Turkey**   www.biramalt.com
Selanik Caddesi, 44/1, TR-Kizilay Ankara
UK: *British Beer & Pub Association*   www.beerandpub.com
Market Towers, 1 Nine Elms Lane, London SW8 5NQ

*Associate member.

Communal Brewing

In the north-eastern part of Bavaria, the historic practice of 'zoigl' brewing continues. In five towns, there are still communal brewhouses, where local people can make beer. The beer is then taken home to be fermented and lagered, and goes on sale in the brewers' own houses. The name zoigl is derived from a corruption of the local word for a sign (the six-pointed brewer's star is displayed to show when beer is on sale).

CAMRA's National Clubs of the Year

1986	ICI Recreation Club, Huddersfield, West Yorkshire
1987–8	West Herts Social Club, Watford, Hertfordshire
1989	St Teresa's Parish Social Centre, Pentworth, Lancashire
1990	No event
1991	ICI Recreation Club, Huddersfield, West Yorkshire
1992	No event
1993	Galleywood Social Club, Galleywood, Essex
1994–5	Appleton Thorne Village Hall, Warrington, Cheshire
1996	No event
1997	Howerd Club, Eltham, London
1998	Ouse Amateur Sailing Club, Ouse, Norfolk
1999	Wakefield Labour Club, Wakefield, West Yorkshire/ Rushden Historical Transport Society Club, Rushden, Northamptonshire (joint)
2000–2	Somer's Sports and Social Club, Halesowen, West Midlands
2003	No event
2004	Sebastopol Social Club, Sebastopol, Torfaen, Wales
2005	The Hastings Club, Lytham St Anne's, Lancashire
2006	Dartford Working Men's Club, Dartford, Kent
2007	Greetland Community & Sporting Association, Halifax, West Yorkshire
2008	Leyton Orient Supporters Club, London/Appleton Thorn Village Hall, Warrington, Cheshire (joint)
2009	Guiseley Factory Workers Club, Guiseley, West Yorkshire
2010	Rushden Historical Transport Society Club, Rushden, Northamptonshire

Although the contest has run continuously, the judging procedure has occasionally extended over more than one calendar year, and a winner has not been announced every year.

Methods of Dispensing Cask Ale

The *Good Beer Guide* recommends four methods of dispensing cask ale that are acceptable to CAMRA. The first is by gravity straight from the cask. The second is by handpump. The third is by gas-, electric- or mechanically-powered pump (no gas in contact with the beer) and the fourth is by air pressure, a system traditionally employed in Scotland.

Buildings Converted to Pubs by Wetherspoon

The JD Wetherspoon pub company has become known for reviving old, often large, town-centre premises by turning them into pubs. Some good examples of its successful building conversions are listed below.

Building Type	*Example Pub*
Amusement arcade	The Mechanical Elephant, Margate
Argos store	The Arthur Robertson, Perry Barr, Birmingham
Assembly rooms	The Assembly Rooms, Epsom
Ballroom	Hamilton Hall, Liverpool Street Station, London
Bank	The Bank Statement, Swansea
Bed shop	The Alfred Herring, Palmer's Green, London
Bingo hall	The Hippodrome, March
Brewery (Wards)	The Sheaf Island, Sheffield
Car factory	The Rodboro Buildings, Guildford
Charity shop (YMCA)	The Broken Bridge, Pontefract
Church	The Earl of Zetland, Grangemouth
Cinema	The Moon Under Water, Manchester
Conservative club	The Bourtree, Hawick
Corn exchange	The Corn Exchange, Arbroath
Courthouse	The Court House, Mansfield
Department store	The Square Peg, Birmingham
Fire station	The Fire Station, Whitley Bay
Gentlemen's club	The Commercial Rooms, Bristol
Market hall	The Old Market Hall, Mexborough
Methodist chapel	Chapel an Gansblydhen, Bodmin
Opera House	The Opera House, Tunbridge Wells
Post office	The Duke's Head, Leominster
Rock club (The Marquee)	The Moon Under Water, Charing Cross, London
Snooker club	The Foot of the Walk, Leith, Edinburgh
Supermarket	The Picture House, Ebbw Vale
Swimming baths	The Sir Titus Salt, Bradford
Theatre	The Playhouse, Colchester
Woolworth's store	JJ Moon's, Ruislip Manor, London

The German Beer Purity Law

Known more simply as the German Beer Purity Law, the Reinheitsgebot, proclaimed in the town of Ingolstadt on 23 April 1516, by Duke Wilhelm IV of Bavaria, restricts the ingredients which can be used to produce beer in Germany to barley, hops and water (wheat – for weissbier brewing – was added to the permitted ingredients later and yeast – not yet understood – was not even considered an ingredient at the time). However, the law also initially included price controls that were intended to be rigorously enforced, as this loose translation reveals.

'We hereby proclaim and decree, by authority of our land, that henceforth everywhere in the Duchy of Bavaria, in the country, as well as in our towns and market places, that, from Michaelmas (29 September) until St George's Day (23 April), a mass* or a kopf** of beer is not to be served for more than one Munich pfennig, and from the St George's Day to Michaelmas, the mass should not be sold for more than two pfennigs of the same currency, the kopf for not more than three heller (usually half a pfennig), on pain of the punishment stated below. However, if anyone brews any beer other than Märzen, it shall not be dispensed and sold for more than one pfennig a mass.

Furthermore, we especially decree that henceforth in all our towns, market places and countryside, that no ingredients other than barley, hops and water be used and needed to make any beer. Anyone knowingly ignoring and contravening our threat shall be punished by the Court by having the barrel of beer confiscated, without fail, each time it happens.

However, should an innkeeper buy one, two, or three pails of beer (containing 60 litres) from a brewery in our towns, market places or the countryside, and sell it to the common people, he alone shall be allowed to sell a mass or kopf of beer for one heller more than mentioned above. Furthermore, should there be shortages and price increases of grain – considering harvest times vary in our region – we, the Duchy of Bavaria, reserve the right to prescribe restrictions to this decree for the benefit of all.'

*A litre jug. **A bowl slightly smaller than a mass in quantity.

Great British Beer Festival Venues

The Great British Beer Festival is the Campaign for Real Ale's annual showcase of the best of British cask ales (hundreds on sale), plus some of the best beers from overseas. More than 65,000 visitors attend during the course of the five-day event, which is held in the first or second week of August. The forerunner of the Great British Beer Festival was the Covent Garden Beer Festival, staged in London 9–13 September 1975.

1977–80	Alexandra Palace, London*
1981–2	Queens Hall, Leeds
1983	Bingley Hall, Birmingham
1984	No event
1985–7	Metropole Hotel, Brighton
1988–9	Queens Hall, Leeds
1990	Metropole Hotel, Brighton
1991	Docklands Arena, London
1992–2005	Olympia, London
2006–11	Earl's Court, London

*1980 event held in tents after Alexandra Palace fire.

'Bottle-Conditioned' in Other Languages

How do you tell if a foreign beer is naturally conditioned in the bottle, apart from holding it up to the light and checking for sediment? The answer is to look for the following phrases, which generally appear on labels from the leading bottle-conditioned beer-producing countries.

France/Southern Belgium	sur levure, sur lie, refermentée en bouteille, fermentation en bouteille
Northern Belgium	op gist, hergist in de fles, nagisting in de fles
Germany	mit hefe*, flaschengärung, naturtrüb
Netherlands	op gist, met gist

*Hefefrei and ohne hefe mean 'yeast-free' and therefore the beer is not bottle-conditioned.

Note that some beers (particularly wheat beers) may contain yeast but may be pasteurized.

Epitome of the Style

One for debate. Could these be the prime examples of classic beer styles?

Style	Beer
80/-	Belhaven 80 Shilling
Alt	Zum Uerige Alt
American IPA	Goose Island IPA
American Pale Ale	Sierra Nevada Pale Ale
Baltic Porter	Zywiec Porter
Barley Wine	Fuller's Golden Pride
Belgian Amber	De Koninck
Belgian Strong Golden	Duvel
Berliner Weisse	Berliner Kindl Weisse
Bière de Garde	Jenlain Ambrée
Bitter	Harveys Sussex Best
Bock	Weltenburger Kloster Asam Bock
Brown Ale (strong)	Newcastle Brown Ale
Brown Ale (sweet)	Manns Brown Ale
Doppelbock	Paulaner Salvator
Dortmunder Export	DAB
Dry Stout	Wye Valley Dorothy Goodbody's Wholesome Stout
Dunkel	Kaltenberg König Ludwig Dunkel
ESB	Fuller's ESB
Golden Ale	Exmoor Gold
Gueuze	Cantillon Gueuze
Helles	Augustiner Hell
Imperial Stout	Harveys Imperial Extra Double Stout
IPA	Meantime IPA
Kölsch	Dom Kölsch
Kriek	Boon Oude Kriek
Märzen	Hacker-Pschorr Oktoberfest Märzen
Mild	Moorhouse's Black Cat
Old Ale	Greene King Strong Suffolk
Pale Ale	Marston's Pedigree
Pilsner	Pilsner Urquell
Porter	Meantime London Porter
Rauchbier	Aecht Schlenkerla Rauchbier

Saison	Saison Dupont
Schwarzbier	Köstritzer Schwarzbier
Sour Red	Rodenbach Grand Cru
Sweet/Milk Stout	Mackeson
Trappist/Abbey Blonde	Achel Blond
Trappist/Abbey Dubbel	Westmalle Dubbel
Trappist/Abbey Tripel	Westmalle Tripel
Vienna	Negra Modelo
Weissbier	Schneider Weisse
Weizenbock	Schneider Aventinus
Witbier	Van Steenberge Celis White

Brewery Beer Themes

Many breweries like to base the names of their beers on a given theme. The list below shows some of the ideas selected by British breweries.

Brewery	Theme
Atomic	nuclear terms
Beartown	bears
Box Steam	steam engines
Bryncelyn	Buddy Holly
Cotleigh	birds of prey
Deeside	Scottish/Pictish kings
Derventio	Ancient Rome
Dowbridge	Roman Britain
Freeminer	Forest of Dean mines
Funfair	fairground rides
Fuzzy Duck	Spoonerisms
Glastonbury	Arthurian legend
Goffs	chivalry
Hambleton	horses
Hesket Newmarket	Lake District landmarks
Mallard	ducks
Milton	myths, legends and gods
Moorhouse's	witchcraft
Nelson	naval terms

Brewery	Theme
Old Chimneys	endangered species
Old Dairy	milk bottle caps
Otley	the letter O
Red Rock	coastal terms
Roseland	local birds
Silverstone	motor racing
Spire	music
Storm	meteorological terms
Three Bs	weaving terms
Titanic	RMS Titanic
Triple fff	rock music tracks
Uley	pigs
Ulverston	Laurel & Hardy
Wantsum	Kent history and people
Watermill	dogs
Wolf	wild dogs
Wooden Hand	pirates
Yetman's	colours

The Most Popular Hops

Hop	Country	Alpha Acid*	Main Uses
Admiral	UK	14.8	British ales
Amarillo	US	8.5	American ales
Bramling Cross	UK	6.9	British ales
Cascade	US	5.5	American ales
Centennial	US	10.5	American ales
Challenger	UK	7.5	British ales
Chinook	US	13.0	American ales
Citra	US	12.0	American ales
First Gold	UK	7.0	British ales
Fuggle	UK	4.5	British ales
Galena	US	13.0	American ales
Golding	UK	5.5	British ales
Hallertauer Hersbrucker	Germany	4.5	German lagers
Hallertauer Mittelfrüh	Germany	4.5	German lagers
Liberty	US	4.0	American lagers
Mount Hood	US	6.0	American lagers
Northdown	UK	8.0	British ales
Northern Brewer	UK/US	8.0	British/American ales
Pacific Gem	New Zealand	15.0	New Zealand ales
Perle	US/Germany	8.0	American ales/ German lagers
Phoenix	UK	13.5	British ales
Pioneer	UK	9.0	British ales
Pride of Ringwood	Australia	10.0	Australian lagers
Progress	UK	6.5	British ales
Saaz	Czech Republic	3.5	Pilsners
Savinjski Golding	Slovenia	5.0	British ales
Simcoe	US	13.0	American ales
Spalt	Germany	4.5	German lagers
Target	UK	11.0	British ales
Tettnanger	Germany	4.5	German lagers
Whitbread Golding Variety (WGV)	UK	6.5	British ales
Willamette	US	5.0	American ales

*Alpha acid content, which is an indicator of the bitterness of the hop, varies from crop to crop. The figures given are approximations of general alpha content.

High Profile Beer Competitions

Competition	Type of Beer	Where Held	Frequency
Brewing Industry International Awards	draught/bottle/can	UK	Biennial
Champion Beer of Britain	cask- /bottle-conditioned	UK	Annual
Champion Winter Beer of Britain	cask-conditioned	UK	Annual
European Beer Star	bottle/can	Germany	Annual
Great American Beer Festival	draught/bottle/can	USA	Annual
International Beer Challenge	bottle/can	UK	Annual
SIBA National Brewing Competition	draught/bottled	UK	Annual
World Beer Awards	bottle/can	International	Annual
World Beer Cup	bottle/can	USA	Biennial

CAMRA's Champion Beers of Scotland and Wales

	Scotland	Wales
1996	Caledonian 80/-	Plassey Dragon's Breath
1997	Caledonian 80/-	Plassey Dragon's Breath
1998	Caledonian Deuchars IPA	Flannery's Oatmeal Stout
1999	Harviestoun Bitter & Twisted	Bullmastiff Gold
2000	Orkney Dark Island	Bullmastiff Gold
2001	Inveralmond Ossian's Ale	Tomos Watkin Merlin's Stout
2002	Harviestoun Bitter & Twisted	Bryncelyn Buddy Marvellous
2003	Orkney Dark Island	Bryncelyn Oh Boy
2004	Cairngorm Trade Winds	Breconshire Golden Valley
2005	Cairngorm Black Gold	Bullmastiff Son of a Bitch
2006	Kelburn Cart Blanche	Otley O8
2007	Highland Dark Munro	Rhymney Dark
2008	Highland Scapa Special	Otley O8
2009	Orkney Raven Ale	Purple Moose Snowdonia Ale
2010	Highland Orkney Blast	Otley O-Garden
2011	Isle of Skye Cuillin Beast	Rhymney Dark

Bottled Beer Conversions

American bottled beers come in strange sizes for those used to quaffing on the other side of the Atlantic. Here are some rough size conversions.

US Fluid Ounces	Ml	US Fluid Ounces	Ml
11.2	330	24	710
12	355	25.4	750
16	473	33.8	1 litre
22*	650		

*Called a 'bomber'; measure often displayed as 1 pint 6 fluid ounces.

Pop Tracks Used in Beer Commercials

Track (Artist)	Beer
Ain't Too Proud to Beg (Temptations)	Budweiser
Albatross (Fleetwood Mac)	Heineken/Lamot Pils
Chelsea Dagger (Fratellis)	Amstel Light
From a Jack to a King (Ned Miller)	Heineken
Galvanize (Chemical Brothers)	Budweiser Select
Guaglione (Perez Prado)	Guinness
Happy Together (Turtles)	Heineken
He Ain't Heavy, He's My Brother (Hollies)	Miller Lite
High Hopes (Frank Sinatra)	Murphy's
I Heard It Through the Grapevine (Marvin Gaye)	Carling Black Label
I Want You (Bob Dylan)	Grolsch
Je T'aime Moi Non Plus (Jane Birkin and Serge Gainsbourg)	John Smith's Bitter
Let it Out (Let It All Hang Out) (Hombres)	Foster's Twist
Love Train (O'Jays)	Coors Light
Raining in My Heart (Buddy Holly)	Heineken
Rhythm of Life (Sammy Davis, Jr)	Guinness
Stop the Cavalry (Jona Lewie)	John Smith's Bitter
The Great Pretender (Platters)	Heineken
Tracks of My Tears (Smokey Robinson and the Miracles)	Budweiser
We Have All the Time in the World (Louis Armstrong)	Guinness
Wipeout (Surfaris)	Guinness
You're So Good To Me (Beach Boys)	Heineken

Roll Out the Barrel

Although it appears to be intrinsically British, the drinking anthem 'Roll Out the Barrel' is in fact a Czech polka tune. It was composed in 1927 by Jaromír Vejvoda and quickly became an international success, generally under the name of 'Beer Barrel Polka'. As such, it was a minor American hit for singer Bobby Vinton in 1975. Earlier, the tune had been adopted by Watney's in the UK as the music for its Red Barrel TV commercials.

Recommended Beer Serving Temperatures

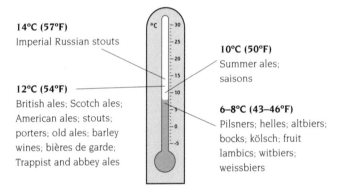

14°C (57°F)
Imperial Russian stouts

10°C (50°F)
Summer ales; saisons

12°C (54°F)
British ales; Scotch ales; American ales; stouts; porters; old ales; barley wines; bières de garde; Trappist and abbey ales

6–8°C (43–46°F)
Pilsners; helles; altbiers; bocks; kölsch; fruit lambics; witbiers; weissbiers

Maltese Beer: The Reading Connection

Malta's best-known brewery is commonly known as Farsons. It is noted for producing top-fermented (ale) beers, when most Mediterranean brewers focus on lager. This is a legacy of the company's founding, when Simonds of Reading, England, which already exported beer to Malta, to quench the thirst of British soldiers stationed on the island, joined forces with the local Farrugia & Sons brewery. Simonds itself no longer exists. Taken over by Courage in 1960, its Reading brewery closed in the early 1980s, but its heritage is not forgotten. The full name of Farsons today is Simonds Farsons Cisk and the Simonds hop leaf emblem is honoured in the name of a strong bitter based on old Simonds recipes.

Czech Beer Numbers

Ever been confused by the number shown on a Czech beer bottle? A beer proudly declared as being 10° sounds daunting but in actual fact only works out at about 4% alcohol by volume. That is because many Czech brewers use the Balling system to calculate the approximate final strength of a beer, just as brewers in other countries have traditionally used original gravity for the same purpose (see page 8). Even though it is no longer a legal requirement to declare beers in this way, most Czech breweries still produce a 10°, 11° (roughly 4.4% ABV) and 12° (5%) beer.

The Five Classic Bottle-Conditioned Beers

At the time of CAMRA's inception in 1971, it is believed only five beers that enjoyed a secondary fermentation in the bottle remained in regular production. The most recent edition of CAMRA's *Good Bottled Beer Guide*, which highlights all known bottle-conditioned beers produced in the UK, features more than 1,300 different beers. The five 'classics' were:

> Courage Imperial Russian Stout*
> Eldridge Pope Thomas Hardy's Ale*
> Gale's Prize Old Ale**
> Guinness Extra Stout*
> Worthington's White Shield***

*No longer in production. **Now brewed by Fuller's. ***Now owned by Molson Coors.

Cicerones and Beer Sommeliers

Proof that the restaurant world is finally taking beer seriously can be found in America's Cicerone programme, run by beer writer Ray Daniels. Aimed at hospitality and catering workers, the independent scheme examines those serving beer, with official Cicerone status awarded to those who truly understand their products, from stocking and presenting to flavours and heritage. The term 'cicerone' more widely refers to a guide to the antiquities and curiosities of places, but now the history, culture and idiosyncrasies of beer are covered by the title, too. The UK's Beer Academy launched its own similar Beer Sommelier scheme in 2011.

A Dozen Great British Beer Shops

1 **Beer-Ritz**, Victoria Buildings, Weetwood Lane, Headingley, Leeds, West Yorkshire LS16 5LX. Tel. 0113 275 3464 www.beerritz.co.uk

2 **Beers of Europe**, Garage Lane, Setchey, King's Lynn, Norfolk PE33 0BE. Tel. 01553 812000 www.beersofeurope.co.uk

3 **Bitter Virtue**, 70 Cambridge Road, Portswood, Southampton, Hampshire SO14 6US. Tel. 023 8055 4881 www.bittervirtue.co uk

4 **Dr.Ink of Fulham**, 349 Fulham Palace Road, London SW6 6TB. Tel. 020 7610 6795 www.drinkoffulham.com

5 **Favourite Beers**, 105 Hewlett Road, Cheltenham, Gloucestershire GL52 6BB. Tel. 01242 220485 www.favouritebeers.com

6 **Green Valley Cyder at Darts Farm**, Clyst St George, Exeter, Devon EX3 0QH. Tel. 01392 876658

7 **Hogs Back Brewery Shop**, Manor Farm, The Street, Tongham, Surrey GU10 1DE. Tel. 01252 783000 www.hogsback.co.uk

8 **The Real Ale Shop**, Branthill Farm, Wells-next-the-Sea, Norfolk NR23 1SB. Tel. 01328 710810 www.therealaleshop.co.uk

9 **Southwick Brewhouse**, Southwick, Fareham, Hampshire PO17 6EB. Tel. 023 92 201133 www.southwickbrewhouse.co.uk

10 **Tucker's Maltings**, Teign Road, Newton Abbot, Devon TQ12 4AA. Tel. 01626 334734 www.tuckersmaltings.com

11 **Utobeer**, Unit 24, Borough Market, London SE1 1TL (open Friday pm and Saturday only). Tel. 020 7394 8601 www.utobeer.com

12 **Westholme Store**, 26 Wallingford Road, Goring-on-Thames, Oxfordshire RG8 0BG. Tel. 01491 872619 www.beersnale.co.uk

For an extensive list of bottled beer shops, see CAMRA's *Good Bottled Beer Guide*.

150 Perfect Places to Have a Beer

In 2008, All About Beer magazine published a list compiled by Rick Lyke of '125 Places to Have a Beer Before You Die'. The feature prompted a huge response and, two years later, Rick re-drew the list to take into account the views of readers. All About Beer published the revised list as '150 Perfect Places to Have a Beer'. Here are Rick's selections (with a few replacements to cover establishments that have subsequently closed).

1   Great American Beer Festival, Denver, Colorado, USA
2   Augustinerkeller, Munich, Germany
3   Abbaye de Notre-Dame d'Orval, Orval, Belgium
4   Monk's Cafe, Philadelphia, Pennsylvania, USA
5   Great British Beer Festival, Earl's Court, London, UK
6   Schlenkerla Heller-Bräu Trum, Bamberg, Germany
7   Horse Brass Pub, Portland, Oregon, USA
8   Kulminator, Antwerp, Belgium
9   Hopleaf Bar, Chicago, Illinois, USA
10 Toronado, San Francisco, California, USA
11 Zum Uerige, Dusseldorf, Germany
12 The Market Porter, London, UK
13 Oregon Brewers Festival, Portland, Oregon, USA
14 U Fleků, Prague, Czech Republic
15 Andechs Monastery, Andechs, Germany
16 Falling Rock Tap House, Denver, Colorado, USA
17 Früh am Dom, Cologne, Germany
18 The Bull & Castle, Dublin, Ireland
19 Oktoberfest, Munich, Germany
20 Brouwer's Cafe, Seattle, Washington, USA
21 Spuyten Duyvil, Brooklyn, New York, USA
22 Brick Store Pub, Decatur, Georgia, USA
23 Cantillon Brewery and Gueuze Museum, Brussels, Belgium
24 Brauhaus Sion, Cologne, Germany
25 Henry's 12th Street Tavern, Portland, Oregon, USA
26 The Ginger Man, Austin, Texas. USA
27 t'Bruges Beertje, Bruges, Belgium
28 Ebenezer's Pub & Restaurant, Lovell, Maine, USA
29 Bruxellensis Festival of Characterful Beers, Brussels, Belgium
30 The Flying Saucer, North/South Carolina, Tennessee, Missouri, Arkansas and Texas, USA
31 d.b.a., New York, USA
32 Kaffe de Hopduvel, Ghent, Belgium

72 Blind Tiger Ale House,
New York, USA

73 The Brewer's Art, Baltimore,
Maryland, USA

74 Birreria l'Orso Elettrico, Rome,
Italy

75 Pivovarský Klub, Prague,
Czech Republic

76 Stumbling Monk, Seattle,
Washington, USA

77 Belgo Central, London, UK

78 Anchor Brewing Co. Tasting
Room, San Francisco,
California, USA

79 Eulogy Belgian Tavern,
Philadelphia, Pennsylvania, USA

80 't Arendsnest, Amsterdam,
Netherlands

81 The Gravity Bar, Guinness
St James's Gate Brewery,
Dublin, Ireland

82 The Australian Hotel, Sydney,
Australia

83 Zlý Časy, Prague,
Czech Republic

84 Cooter Brown's, New Orleans,
Louisiana, USA

85 Delirium Café, Brussels,
Belgium

86 Ye Olde Mitre Tavern, London,
UK

87 Delilah's, Chicago, Illinois, USA

88 Deschutes Brewery & Public
House, Bend, Oregon, USA

89 Mahar's, Albany, New York, USA

90 Armsby Abbey, Worcester,
Massachusetts, USA

91 Dogfish Head Ale House,
Rehoboth Beach, Delaware, USA

92 Sail and Anchor, Fremantle,
Australia

93 Mecklenburg Gardens,
Cincinnati, Ohio, USA

94 The Map Room, Chicago,
Illinois, USA

95 The Publick House, Brookline,
Massachusetts, USA

96 Gosenschenke Ohne
Bedenken, Leipzig, Germany

97 Holiday Ale Festival, Portland,
Oregon, USA

98 Olympen Mat & Vinhus, Oslo,
Norway

99 O'Brien's Pub, San Diego,
California, USA

100 Antares Palermo,
Buenos Aires, Argentina

101 Bierproeflokaal In de Wildeman,
Amsterdam, Netherlands

102 Beerbistro, Toronto, Ontario,
Canada

103 Charlie's Bar, Copenhagen,
Denmark

104 McSorley's Old Ale House,
New York, USA

105 Die Weisse, Salzburg, Austria

106 Irseer Klosterbräu, Irsee,
Germany

107 Max's Taphouse, Baltimore,
Maryland, USA

108 McMenamins Kennedy School
Hotel, Portland, Oregon, USA

109 Chez Moeder Lambic, Brussels,
Belgium

110 Sunset Grill & Tap, Boston,
Massachusetts, USA

111 James E McNellie's Public
House, Tulsa, Oklahoma, USA

112 PINT Bokbierfestival,
Amsterdam, Netherlands

113 Redbones, Somerville,
Massachusetts, USA

114 Sleeping Lady Brewing Co./
Snow Goose Restaurant,
Anchorage, Alaska, USA

115 Russian River Brewing Co.,
Santa Rosa, California, USA

116 The Happy Gnome, St. Paul,
Minnesota, USA

117 Milltown, Carrboro,
North Carolina, USA

118 Zythos Bier Festival,
Leuven, Belgium

119 Thirsty Monk, Asheville,
North Carolina, USA

120 Goose Island Brewpub,
Chicago, Illinois, USA

121 Sierra Nevada Brewing Co.,
Chico, California, USA

122 Moan and Dove, Amherst,
Massachusetts, USA

123 Neuzeller Kloster Bräu,
Neuzelle, Germany

124 Kelham Island Tavern,
Sheffield, UK

125 Taco Mac, branches in Georgia
and Tennessee, USA

126 American Flatbread Burlington
Hearth, Burlington, Vermont,
USA

127 The White Horse,
Parson's Green, London, UK

128 Tinkoff, Moscow, Russia

129 5 Seasons Brewing Co.,
Atlanta, Georgia, USA

130 The Church Brew Works,
Pittsburgh, Pennsylvania, USA

131 Alibi Room, Vancouver,
British Columbia, Canada

132 Gösser Bierklinik, Vienna,
Austria

133 Stockholm Beer & Whisky
Festival, Stockholm, Sweden

134 The Bell, Aldworth, Berkshire, UK

135 Brouwerij 't IJ, Amsterdam,
Netherlands

136 TY Harbor Brewery, Tokyo,
Japan

137 The Hart & Thistle, Halifax,
Nova Scotia, Canada

138 Ye Olde Cheshire Cheese,
London, UK

139 Sugar Maple, Milwaukee,
Wisconsin, USA

140 Mitchell's Waterfront Brewery
& Scottish Ale House,
Cape Town, South Africa

141 Kelly's Caribbean Bar, Grill &
Brewery, Key West, Florida, USA

142 Cole's Restaurant, Buffalo,
New York, USA

143 Heineken Brewery, Amsterdam,
Netherlands

144 The Dubliner, Washington, DC,
USA

145 Matt Brewing Co. Tasting
Room, Utica, New York, USA

146 Shakespeare Brewery & Hotel,
Auckland, New Zealand

147 Boxing Cat Brewery, Shanghai,
China

148 Old Ebbitt Grill,
Washington, DC, USA

149 Bar 35, Honolulu, Hawaii, USA

150 Mr Sancho's Beach, Cozumel,
Mexico

Common UK Beer Bottle Sizes

275 ml; 330 ml; 500 ml; 568 ml (1 pint);
660 ml; 750 ml; 2 litre (PET)

A Strong Beer Snapshot

Beer (ABV)	Brewery
The End of History (55%)	BrewDog, UK (2010)
Schorschbock (43%)	Schorschbräu, Germany
Tactical Nuclear Penguin (32%)	BrewDog, UK (2009)
Samuel Adams Utopias (27%)	Boston Beer, USA
Baz's Super Brew (23%)	Parish, UK (mid-1990s)
Uncle Igor's (21%)	Ross, UK (mid-1990s)
120 Minute IPA (20%+)	Dogfish Head, USA
Samuel Adams MMM (19.5–20%)	Boston Beer, USA (1999)
Raison d'Extra (18%+)	Dogfish Head, USA
Worldwide Stout (18%+)	Dogfish Head, USA
Samuel Adams Triple Bock (18%)	Boston Beer, USA
Dark Lord (15%)	Three Floyds, USA
Olde School Barleywine (15%)	Dogfish Head, USA
Farrier's Bitter (14%)	Shoes, UK
Samichlaus (14%)	Eggenberger, Austria
Bezelbuth (13%)	Grain d'Orge, France
Aventinus Weizen-Eisbock (12%)	Schneider, Germany
Baz's Bonce Blower (12%)	Parish, UK
Edwin Tucker's Victorian Stock Ale (12%)	Teignworthy, UK (late-1990s)
Thomas Hardy's Ale (11.7%)	Eldridge Pope (1968–1999)/ O'Hanlon's, UK (2000s)

Beers are still available, unless otherwise dated.

Gay Beer

Mexico's Minerva brewery offers two honey-infused beers specifically targeted at the gay/lesbian market. Purple Hand Beer (named after a gay rights protest in San Francisco in 1969) and Salamandra both have detachable labels so that they can be worn as a symbol of gay pride.

National Maximum Permitted Blood Alcohol Levels for Driving

Grams/100 ml	Country
0.00	Czech Republic, Hungary, Panama, Romania, Russia, Slovak Republic
0.02	Brazil, China, Croatia, Estonia, Norway, Poland, Sweden
0.03	Japan
0.04	Colombia, Lithuania
0.05	Argentina, Australia, Austria, Belgium, Bulgaria, Chile, Costa Rica, Cyprus, Denmark, Dominican Republic, Finland, France, Germany*, Greece, Italy, Latvia, Luxembourg, Netherlands, Peru, Portugal, Slovenia, South Africa, South Korea, Spain, Switzerland, Turkey
0.07	Honduras
0.08	Canada, Ecuador, Guatemala**, Ireland, Malta, Mexico, New Zealand, UK, USA, Venezuela
0.10	El Salvador

*0.03 when involved in an accident, endangering or hurting someone.

**Prosecution may result at 0.05 where driver is incapacitated.

Source: Worldwide Brewing Alliance Drinking and Driving Report 2008.

John Barleycorn Must Die

The title of a 1970 album by Traffic, *John Barleycorn Must Die* refers to an ancient British folk song, with versions penned by Robert Burns, among others. In the song, the crop barley is assigned human qualities and is brutally treated. His abusers first of all plough him into the ground, then he rises up and becomes strong until they hack him down and take him away to a place where he is soaked in water, cast upon a floor and then scorched with flame. Next, a miller takes his turn to inflict punishment, grinding him between stones. But John Barleycorn is a great survivor, his 'blood', when consumed, helping the working man forget his troubles. Apart from Traffic, the song has been recorded by such performers as Fairport Convention, Steeleye Span and Jethro Tull.

The Four Founders of CAMRA

Michael Hardman   Graham Lees   Jim Makin   Bill Mellor

CAMRA, the Campaign for Real Ale, was established in 1971 by four friends who shared a pessimistic view of how the UK brewing industry was changing. They set up a consumer organisation – initially titled the Campaign for the Revitalisation of Ale – to contest the power of the big breweries and to preserve the best traditions of the brewing and pub industries. Four decades on, CAMRA has more than 125,000 members.

A Chronology of Notable US Brewery Openings

1829	Yuengling	1987	Full Sail
1845	Minhas	1988	Deschutes
1855	Miller*		Great Lakes
1857	Stevens Point		Goose Island**
1860	Anheuser-Busch**		Rogue
	August Schell	1989	Boulevard
1861	Iron City		Long Trail
1863	Pabst***		Odell
1873	Coors*	1990	Flying Dog
1888	Matt	1991	New Belgium
1896	Anchor	1993	Lagunitas
1909	Spoetzl		Left Hand
1979	Sierra Nevada		New Glarus
1983	Mendocino	1994	Great Divide
1984	BridgePort		Kona
1985	Bell's		Shipyard
	Boston Beer Company	1995	Dogfish Head
1986	Abita	1996	Firestone Walker
	Alaskan		Stone
	Harpoon		Victory
	Summit	1997	Russian River
1987	Brooklyn		Sweetwater

*Now part of MillerCoors.

**Now part of A-B InBev.

***No brewery: beers now brewed under contract.

146

Poetic Taste of Beer

'I liked the taste of the beer, its live, white lather, its brass-bright depth,
the sudden world through the wet brown walls of the glass,
the tilted rush to the lips and the slow swallowing down to the
lapping belly, the salt on the tongue, the foam at the corners.'

Old Garbo, Dylan Thomas

Unusual Wheat Beers

Hidden for years behind the Iron Curtain, and declared extinct by some
observers, a trio of wheat beer styles are now slowly coming back to life.
They remain extremely rare finds, so drink them while (or if) you can!

Style	Country	Description
Gose	Germany	Wheat beer seasoned with salt and coriander
Grätzer/Grodziskie	Poland	Smoked wheat beer
Lichtenhainer	Germany	Acidic smoked wheat beer

'Cheers!' in Other Languages

Language	Translation	Language	Translation
Bulgarian	na zdrave!	Hungarian	egészségére!
Chinese	gan bei!	Italian	salute/cin cin!
Croatian	živjeli!	Japanese	kanpai!
Czech	na zdraví!	Latvian	priekā!
Danish	skål!	Lithuanian	buk sveikas!
Dutch	proost!	Norwegian	skål!
Esperanto	je via sano!	Polish	na zdrowie!
Estonian	terviseks!	Portuguese	saúde!
Finnish	kippis!	Romanian	noroc!
French	santé!	Russian	na zdorovie!
Gaelic	sláinte!	Spanish	salud!
German	prost!	Swedish	skål!
Greek	yamas!	Welsh	iechyd da!

Further Reading

Below is a selection of influential, important, useful and entertaining books on beer, some still in print, others requiring more effort to find.

100 *Belgian Beers to Try Before You Die!*, Tim Webb & Joris Pattyn (CAMRA Books, 2008)

300 *Beers to Try Before You Die!*, Roger Protz (CAMRA Books, 2005)

500 *Beers*, Zak Avery (Apple, 2010)

1001 *Beers You Must Try Before You Die*, editor Adrian Tierney-Jones (Cassell, 2010)

The Ale Trail, Roger Protz (Dobby, 1995)

Amber Gold & Black, Martyn Cornell (History Press, 2010)

An Appetite for Ale, Fiona Beckett & Will Beckett (CAMRA Books, 2007)

Around Amsterdam/Berlin/Bruges/Brussels/London in 80 Beers, various authors (Cogan & Mater, various years)

The Bedside Book of Beer, Barrie Pepper (Alma Books, 1990)

Beer, Michael Jackson (Dorling Kindersley, 1998)

Beer (*Eyewitness Guide*), various authors (Dorling Kindersley, 2007)

Beer, The Story of the Pint, Martyn Cornell (Headline, 2003)

A Beer a Day, Jeff Evans (CAMRA Books, 2008)

Beer and Skittles, Richard Boston (Collins, 1976)

The Beer Book, Tim Hampson (Dorling Kindersley, 2008)

Beer Companion, Michael Jackson (Mitchell Beazley, 1993)

The Beer Cookbook, Susan Nowak (Faber & Faber, 1999)

The Beer Drinker's Companion, Frank Baillie (David & Charles, 1975)

Beer for Pete's Sake, Pete Slosberg (Siris Books, 1998)

Beer Glorious Beer, editors Barrie Pepper and Roger Protz (Quiller, 2000)

The Beer Lover's Guide to the USA, Stan Hieronymus and Daria Labinsky (St Martin's Griffin, 2000)

Beers of North America, Bill Yenne (Longmeadow, 1986)

The Big Book of Beer, Adrian Tierney-Jones (CAMRA Books, 2005)

The Brewery Manual, editor Larry Nelson (Advantage, annual)

The Brewing Industry in England, 1700–1830, Peter Mathias (Gregg Revivals, 1993)

Brewing with Wheat, Stan Hieronymus (Brewers Publications, 2010)

The Brewmaster's Table, Garrett Oliver (HarperCollins, 2003)

The British Brewing Industry 1830–1980, TR Gourvish & RG Wilson (Cambridge, 1994)

The CAMRA Guide to London's Best Beer Pubs & Bars, Des de Moor
(CAMRA Books, 2011)

The Complete Joy of Homebrewing, Charlie Papazian (Harper, 2003)

Death of the English Pub, Christopher Hutt (Arrow, 1973)

The Encyclopedia of Beer, editor Christine P Rhodes (Henry Holt, 1995)

The English Pub, Peter Haydon (Hale, 1994: republished as *Beer and
Britannia*, Sutton, 2001)

Good Beer Guide, CAMRA (CAMRA Books, annual)

Good Beer Guide Belgium, Tim Webb (CAMRA Books, 2009)

Good Beer Guide Germany, Steve Thomas (CAMRA Books, 2006)

Good Beer Guide Prague & the Czech Republic, Evan Rail
(CAMRA Books, 2007)

Good Beer Guide West Coast USA, Ben McFarland & Tom Sandham
(CAMRA Books, 2008)

Good Bottled Beer Guide, Jeff Evans (CAMRA Books, 2009)

Great Beer Guide, Michael Jackson (Dorling Kindersley, 2005)

Great Beers of Belgium, Michael Jackson (Brewers Publications, 2008)

The Great British Beer Book, Roger Protz (Impact, 1987)

The Guinness Book of Traditional Pub Games, Arthur Taylor
(Guinness, 1992)

A History of Brewing, HS Corran (David & Charles, 1975)

Hops and Glory, Pete Brown (Macmillan, 2009)

LambicLand, Tim Webb, Chris Pollard & Siobhan McGinn
(Cogan & Mater, 2010)

London by Pub, Ted Bruning (Prion, 2001)

Man Walks into a Pub, Pete Brown (Pan, 2003)

The New World Guide to Beer, Michael Jackson (Apple, 1991)

The Oxford Companion to Beer, editor Garrett Oliver
(Oxford University Press, 2011)

Played at the Pub, Arthur Taylor (English Heritage, 2009)

Prince of Ales, The History of Brewing in Wales, Brian Glover
(Alan Sutton, 1993)

Pulling a Fast One, Roger Protz (Pluto, 1978)

Radical Brewing, Randy Mosher (Brewers Publications, 2004)

The Taste of Beer, Roger Protz (Weidenfeld & Nicolson, 1998)

Tasting Beer, Randy Mosher (Storey, 2009)

Three Sheets to the Wind, Pete Brown (Pan, 2006)

World Beer Guide, Roger Protz (Carlton, 2009)

World's Best Beers, Ben McFarland (Jacqui Small, 2009)

Index

Author's Acknowledgements

The author wishes to thank Iain Loe, CAMRA's Research and Information Manager, for his assistance with this book, and the following people for their input, and apologizes to anyone whose valued contribution may have been inadvertently overlooked: Des de Moor, Chris Garrett, Paul Gatza, Eddie Gershon, Tim Hampson, Malcolm Harding, Stan Hieronymus, Robert Humphreys, Tricia Hurle, Julie Johnson, Yuriy Katunin, Sue Kilner, Rick Lyke, Susan Nowak, Charlie Papazian, Chris Pollard, Rupert Ponsonby, Roger Protz, Evan Rail, David Sheen, Paul Sullivan, Adrian Tierney-Jones, Elisa Trapani, Tim Webb.

Books for Beer Lovers

Good Beer Guide 2012

Editor: Roger Protz

The *Good Beer Guide* is the only guide you will ever need to find the right pint, in the right place, every time. It's the original and best-selling guide to around 4,500 pubs throughout the UK. Now in its 39th year, this annual publication is a comprehensive and informative guide to the best real ale pubs in the UK, researched and written exclusively by CAMRA members and fully updated every year.

£15.99   ISBN 978-1-85249-286-1

Good Bottled Beer Guide

Jeff Evans

A pocket-sized guide for discerning drinkers looking to buy bottled real ales and enjoy a fresh glass of their favourite beers at home. The 7th edition of the *Good Bottled Beer Guide* is completely revised, updated and redesigned to showcase the very best bottled British real ales now being produced, and detail where they can be bought. Everything you need to know about bottled beers; tasting notes, ingredients, brewery details, and a glossary to help the reader understand more about them.

£12.99   ISBN 978-1-85249-262-5

300 Beers to Try Before You Die!

Roger Protz

300 beers from around the world, handpicked by award-winning journalist, author and broadcaster Roger Protz, to try before you die! A comprehensive portfolio of top beers from the smallest microbreweries in the United States to family-run British breweries and the world's largest brands. This book is indispensible for both beer novices and aficionados.

£14.99   ISBN 978-1-85249-273-1

A Beer a Day

Jeff Evans

Written by leading beer writer Jeff Evans, A Beer a Day is a beer lover's almanac, crammed with beers from around the world to enjoy on every day and in every season, and celebrating beer's connections with history, sport, music, film and television. Whether it's Christmas Eve, Midsummer's Day, Bonfire Night, or just a wet Wednesday in the middle of October, A Beer a Day has just the beer for you to savour and enjoy.

£16.99   ISBN 978-1-85249-235-9

London's Best Beer, Pubs & Bars

Des de Moor

London's Best Beer, Pubs & Bars is the essential guide to beer drinking in London. This practical book is packed with detailed maps and easy-to-use listings to help you find the best places to enjoy perfect pints in the capital. Laid out by area, find the best pubs serving the best British and international beers wherever you are. Features tell you more about London's rich history of brewing and the city's vibrant modern brewing scene, where well-known brands rub shoulders with tiny micro-breweries.

£12.99   ISBN 978-1-85249-285-4

Great British Pubs

Adrian Tierney-Jones

Great British Pubs is a celebration of the British pub. This fully illustrated and practical book presents the pub as an ultimate destination. It recommends a selection of the very best pubs in various different categories, as chosen by leading beer writer Adrian Tierney-Jones. Every kind of pub is represented, with full-colour photography helping to showcase a host of excellent pubs from the seaside to the city and from the historic to the ultra-modern.

£14.99   ISBN 978-1-85249-265-6

100 Belgian Beers to Try Before You Die!

Tim Webb & Joris Pattyn

100 Belgian Beers to Try Before You Die! showcases 100 of the best Belgian beers as chosen by internationally-known beer writers Tim Webb and Joris Pattyn. Lavishly illustrated throughout with images of the beers, breweries, Belgian beer bars and some of the characters involved in Belgian brewing, the book encourages both connoisseurs and newcomers to Belgian beer to sample them for themselves, both in Belgium and at home.

£12.99   ISBN 987-1-85249-248-9

Brew Your Own British Real Ale at Home

Graham Wheeler

The perennial favourite of home-brewers, Brew Your Own British Real Ale is a CAMRA classic. This new edition is re-written, enhanced and updated with new recipes for contemporary and award-winning beers, as well as recipes for old favourites no longer brewed commercially. Written by home-brewing authority Graham Wheeler, Brew Your Own British Real Ale includes detailed brewing instructions for both novice and more advanced home-brewers, as well as comprehensive recipes for recreating some of Britain's best-loved beers at home.

£14.99   ISBN 978-1-85249-258-8

Lake District Pub Walks

Bob Steel

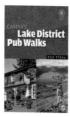

A pocket-sized, traveller's guide to some of the best walking and best pubs in the Lake District. The 30 walks are grouped geographically around tourist hubs with plenty of accommodation, making the book ideal for a visitor to the Lakes. The book is fully illustrated, with clear Ordnance Survey mapping and written directions to help readers navigate the routes.

£9.99   ISBN 978-1-85249-271-7

Order these and other CAMRA books online at **www.camra.org.uk/books**, ask your local bookstore, or contact: CAMRA, 230 Hatfield Road, St Albans, AL1 4LW. Telephone 01727 867201

It takes all sorts to Campaign for Real Ale

CAMRA, the Campaign for Real Ale, is an independent not-for-profit, volunteer-led consumer group. We promote good-quality real ale and pubs, as well as lobbying government to champion drinkers' rights and protect local pubs as centres of community life.

CAMRA has over 125,000 members from all ages and backgrounds, brought together by a common belief in the issues that CAMRA deals with and their love of good quality British beer. From just £20 a year – that's less than a pint a month – you can join CAMRA and enjoy the following benefits:

- A monthly colour newspaper and quarterly magazine informing you about beer and pub news and detailing events and beer festivals around the country.
- Free or reduced entry to over 150 national, regional and local beer festivals.
- Money off many of our publications including the *Good Beer Guide* and the *Good Bottled Beer Guide*.
- A 10% discount on all holidays booked with Cottages4you and a 8% discount on all holidays booked with Thomas Cook online.
- £20 worth of JD Wetherspoon real ale vouchers (40 x 50p off a pint).
- The opportunity to campaign to save pubs under threat of closure, for pubs to be open when people want to drink and a reduction in beer duty that will help Britain's brewing industry survive.

Do you feel passionately about your pint? Then why not join CAMRA?

Just fill in the application form (or a photocopy of it) and the Direct Debit form on the next page to receive 15 months membership for the price of 12!*

If you wish to join but do not want to pay by Direct Debit, please fill in the application form below and send a cheque, payable to CAMRA, to: CAMRA, 230 Hatfield Road, St Albans, Hertfordshire, AL1 4LW. Please note than non Direct Debit payments will incur a £2 surcharge. Figures are given below.

Please tick appropriate box	Direct Debit	Non Direct Debit
Single membership (UK & EU)	£20 ☐	£22 ☐
Concessionary membership (under 26 or 60 and over)	£14 ☐	£16 ☐
Joint membership	£25 ☐	£27 ☐
Concessionary joint membership	£17 ☐	£19 ☐

Life membership information is available on request.

Title _____ Surname _____

Forename(s) _____

Address _____

_____ Postcode _____

Date of Birth _____ Email address _____

CAMRA will occasionally send you e-mails related to your membership. We will also allow your local branch access to your email. If you would like to opt-out of contact from your local branch please tick here ☐ (at no point will your details be released to a third party).

Find out more at www.camra.org.uk/joinus or telephone 01727 867201

*15 months membership for the price of 12 is only available the first time a member pays by Direct Debit.

NOTE: Membership benefits are subject to change.

Instruction to your Bank or Building Society to pay by Direct Debit

DIRECT Debit

Please fill in the form and send to: Campaign for Real Ale Ltd. 230 Hatfield Road, St. Albans, Herts. AL1 4LW

Name and full postal address of your Bank or Building Society

To The Manager _____ Bank or Building Society

Address

Postcode

Name (s) of Account Holder (s)

Bank or Building Society account number

Branch Sort Code

Reference Number

Banks and Building Societies may not accept Direct Debit Instructions for some types of account

Originator's Identification Number

9	2	6	1	2	9

FOR CAMRA OFFICIAL USE ONLY
This is not part of the instruction to your **Bank or Building Society**

Membership Number

Name

Postcode

Instruction to your Bank or Building Society
Please pay CAMRA Direct Debits from the account detailed on this Instruction subject to the safeguards assured by the Direct Debit Guarantee. I understand that this instruction may remain with CAMRA and, if so, will be passed electronically to my Bank/Building Society

Signature(s)

Date

✂ detached and retained this section

DIRECT Debit

This Guarantee should be detached and retained by the payer.

The Direct Debit Guarantee

- This Guarantee is offered by all Banks and Building Societies that take part in the Direct Debit Scheme. The efficiency and security of the Scheme is monitored and protected by your own Bank or Building Society.

- If the amounts to be paid or the payment dates change CAMRA will notify you 10 working days in advance of your account being debited or as otherwise agreed.

- If an error is made by CAMRA or your Bank or Building Society, you are guaranteed a full and immediate refund from your branch of the amount paid.

- You can cancel a Direct Debit at any time by writing to your Bank or Building Society. Please also send a copy of your letter to us.